HEY
MANAGERS
IN THE MIDDLE,
IMPROVE YOUR
THINKING, PLEASE

A SURVIVAL-TO-SUCCESS GUIDE
FOR MANUFACTURING
AND OPERATIONS

T0342586

VINEET AHUJA

Tellwell Talent
www.tellwell.ca

ISBN
978-0-2288-9504-6 (Hardcover)
978-0-2288-9503-9 (Paperback)
978-0-2288-9505-3 (eBook)

TABLE OF CONTENTS

PREFACE

I always wanted to become a business adviser or management consultant to help businesses and their leaders to grow, even when I was at college for engineering. I must say I achieved what I set out to be having gone through the challenges in professional life. The book is written as my contribution to fellow managers who have got stuck in the middle.

My early education was in boarding schools thanks to a Government of India merit scholarship I won when I was six years old. I first studied in Birla Vidya Mandir, Nainital, in northern India, and then in one of the most prestigious Modern School, New Delhi, to finish my higher (senior) secondary schooling in 1970. I then joined Delhi College of Engineering to graduate in Mechanical Engineering in 1975.

From there, my career journey started first in small jobs, then I moved to Indian Oil, the largest oil company in India and one of the most profitable government-owned public company in India (https://iocl.com/). My foundations as a person and as a manager were built over fourteen years with this great company. Having been selected to work in the Technical Services department, I learnt and implemented application engineering across a vast industrial base, across almost every type of industry that you can think of. I spent hours working with the management and floor-level employees of hundreds of companies across Eastern India first and then in Northern

India. My ability to interact with all levels of staff, from the lowest to the highest, is a result of the people skills I developed in this job and then further deliberate upskilling throughout my life. My later studies in the MBA program at the prestigious Faculty of Management Studies, Delhi University, opened my mind to management like no other studies did, and I am especially grateful for the teachers I learnt from in marketing, operational research and financial management.

In 1990, after fourteen years at Indian Oil, I moved to Australia and decided to settle in Melbourne. Finding a job in the oil industry in a similar role was hard, so I decided to change my career path and went into manufacturing. In recession times of 1990 the jobs were not readily available in Melbourne so I first found work selling insurance and then was able to get a job in a small plastics products company whose Managing Director told me not to tell anyone my qualifications and to learn the job from the process floor up. But I was lucky to be recognised for my work and became a supervisor first and then a plant manager in about six months. That was the start of my journey in manufacturing, operations, and finally consulting. During my time with this company, I oversaw a technology transfer project over to a joint venture company in Malaysia but when the company went into receivership in 1992 or so, I was the first one to be let go. This was a pattern I faced a few times in my life in Australia.

In this time I also came across network marketing concept and got into Amway for starting my own business. The business was set up to get a passive income, while working in the jobs I was employed in. The organisation I joined the business through was Network 21 and that really laid my foundations for leadership in setting up my own organisation and on how to run my own small business. The training provided by the various leaders of global Network 21 has been great learnings as it taught me to understand my self, to grow personally, how to handle rejection and grow an income purely by helping those who have a dream but don't know where to start from. Getting an established system to work from and have a great mentoring support of successful leaders "holding your hands to walk you through" has been one of the greatest learnings and character building. Over the years this has given me a great passive income and continues to provide.

I worked at another small company before I was able to join a multinational hygiene chemical company as Assistant Plant Manager. In this period, I also finished my post-graduate diploma in Quality Management from RMIT Melbourne. From here I was picked up into another multinational, which was beginning of a "J"-curve success in my career, as I grew from an Efficiency Improvement Engineer to become a Manufacturing Manager, then International Projects Manager in a short period of two years. During this period, I set up a problem-solving team in a two-shift operations work centre to eliminate a long-term inefficient production and resultant perennial back-order problem for a major product. That success led to more teams and influenced continuous improvement work at the larger site where my colleague also took on the conversion so we helped convert three units to team structures, affecting total culture change, which even the unions appreciated. So, from one successful team we had various work centres on teams across the multiple units on site. The Managing Director then asked me to move to a loss-making unit at another site to convert to profit making within 1.5 years maximum. I identified serious work safety problem (a very large % people had reported work-related injuries) and a huge morale problem. Again, the success came by changing to a TEAMs structure, encouraging workers from floor to take on team leadership roles and mentoring them. We saw that running sites with self-managed teams brought about cultural change company-wide, a trend that continued as I moved my expertise into roles at other companies. This period of my career is a source of pride for me, as my contribution to improvements and the changes I made really made a difference in the life of the people I led and the companies I managed. This period also helped hone my skills. The multinational company where I achieved all this success closed their operations in Australia, so I helped with its technology transfers to international locations post-closure, eventually coming back to Australia.

I then worked in Australian-owned companies and that is where I made my first foray into consulting, which included project management and developing business for U.S.-based IT companies that were selling their technologies in Australia (achieved business from Telstra). I got an opportunity to run my own business, too, when I joined a friend in taking over almost dying small chocolate confectionary company as a Manufacturing Director. We revived the business, but I moved away from my role after two-and-a-half years as I felt I needed more out my career than that as minority partner in a very small company. But that experience was great, and the business still is operative, being run by my ex-partner.

My experience in food manufacturing at the chocolate company helped me in my work as a Production Coach/ Production Manager/Factory Manager/Operations Manager over the next decade and so in different companies. In these places, I created opportunities to improve productivity and costs, but mainly I was building staff development and engagement. My principle of RAAT as shown in Rule 6 (Responsibility Authority, Accountability and Trust) has always been my process for building staff engagement and changing culture. There is a great feeling one gets when we see people from the floor take on higher roles and execute them with pride and finesse. Daily firefighting does not need any intervention by a middle manager. When the manager can trust employees to make decisions, it frees up time for management. Employees can go ahead and solve the day-to-day issues by consulting within the team and only go to the manager for decisions needing guidelines or policy.

But life kept teaching me lessons. I was victim of restructuring and cost cutting and let go as a factory manager. After another short stint as a plant manager in a pet food manufacturing, I became a project manager helping set up a joint venture plant, then operations manager for a health food company.

After a total of almost 37 years, I again took up consulting in the operations and manufacturing arena, first in one of my previous companies (my ex- factory manager role), which called me back to fix major problems and get out of rot developed, since I had left, and then at another company that needed me to implement continuous improvement training and a staff assessment project on sub-contract in Mondelez-Kraft Foods.

The consulting assignments led me to a business advisor role, where I worked with small and medium enterprises (SMEs) in a government-run programme called Enterprise Connect (later on called the Entrepreneurs Programme), which was set up to provide assistance and grant funds to help SMEs grow. Over almost nine years, I worked with over 120 companies in manufacturing, transport, food processing, agri-food, poultry, retail, distribution, engineering, packaging, export, health care, management services, many types of beverages, hydroponics, irrigation, nutraceuticals, design engineering, innovations, plastics, compost, air conditioning, IT, fashion, catering, solar, hearing aids, LED lighting designs, recycling/ circular economy, radiology services, electronics, health foods etc. Some of my proud achievements are as below:

- Provided advice and assistance to companies in improving their operations, reducing costs, improving profits, export, and restructuring to get government incentives. Among my experiences, there are many examples of multiplying revenue, increasing profit (EBIT/EBITDA and improve value addition %, and many case studies have been written of businesses who have gained from my engagement. Amongst my many achievements, I will just give two examples. In the first, I transformed the thinking of a major national SME to improve EBIT by almost 50%. In the second, my contribution multiplied the revenue of a pasta manufacturer by 2.78 times to become a major player in Australia. There are many more stories like this.

- Assisted businesses in accessing total of millions of $ grants from the Commonwealth Government and State Government for capital expansion. Over the past few years, I have helped a lot of SMEs scale up manufacturing and grow their capacities and capabilities to multiply revenue, profits, and cash flow.

- Inspired CEOs to grow personally and to understand and implement "working on the business" rather than "in the business"; to change the culture from "tax minimisation" to "profit maximisation"; and to apply for regular funding through R&D tax incentives and Export Market Development Grants etc.

- Assisted change of culture, improved morale, and developed self-managed teams. In my work, I used established confidential employee surveys and help resolve the identified issues across organisations.

- Set up and ran advisory boards to improve effectiveness and accountability for the owners and directors. I am blessed that when I decided to retire from full time role, many businesses CEOs wanted me to continue advising them and so I am kept busy.

- Analysed key company data, such as financial, operational, costings, sales and staffing numbers, to help benchmark companies against others in their industry and strive for best in class.
- Developed second-tier leadership conducting workshops on business plans, value propositions etc and helped build skill and knowledge strategies for future.
- Set up specific key performance measures across the business for effective control and monitoring.

All these experiences totaling around 47 years plus total were blood, sweat and hard work and my obsession to improve business practices, motivate people to grow to their potential and growing the businesses. This keen interest is the reason to write this book so that I can leave a legacy of my experience, successes, failures and knowledge to the new generation of managers to improve their own careers and so inspire their next generation. If I can contribute to make life better for them, I have made some contribution to the humanity!

ACKNOWLEDGEMENTS

I wish to thank many people who have taught, mentored, straightened, corrected and enriched me to become capable to write the book. I can't mention all those who affected me as there are so many, so if you feel you contributed but I have missed you, then please forgive me. I wish to especially acknowledge:

Business leaders like late Jim Dornan and Nancy Dornan, Mitch and Diedrie Sala, Prem and Geeta Pillay, my sister Rashmi and husband Sushil Pachnanda – they have contributed so much to my learning.

My peers/mentors in Australia: Bruno Bello, Gus Cantone, Keith Stanney, David Schloeffel, Vivian Felling, Greg Chalker, Rod Nelson, Prof Amrik Sohal, Bruce Rutter who all helped me achieve what I set out to.

My school and college friends: late Sameer Mathur, Shubhabrata Bhattacharya, Sanjeev Kapoor, Ravinder Kumar Gupta, Vinod Taneja, Ravi Bharadwaj who all have provided a long-lasting friendship support. Koshika Foundation founders Sunil Tandon, Somesh Sehgal, Anil Sachdeva who since college were close and now even closer in a common cause.

My close friends from Melbourne, Australia who are family - Mohinder Singh Pannu, Rajiv Gulati, Ravi Lakhani, Vijay Rao, Anup & Reena Tandon and so many others in the groups. Also, every one in the Sunday coffee group especially Deepak Maini, Sunil Khare, Vijay Wardhan.

My close friends from Indian Oil – Ranchod Yagnik, C.P. Joshi, Vinay Kumar, Rakesh Sarin, B Laxminarayan and so many others that have been there to guide and support,

My 120+ clients with whom I worked as Business Adviser with and hopefully left a legacy.

My wife Roma without whose critique nothing in my life would have happened. Credit goes to our daughter Manasi, son Rohan and their respective spouses Ujwal and Kaajal for keeping us relevant.

And all those who came into my life over the past six plus decades- forgive me if I may have slipped to mention directly.

INTRODUCTION

You are a middle manager in an organisation, perhaps at a lower level, maybe at mid-level, or even at senior level, but you feel stuck in the cycle of corporate growth, dependent upon your boss whose decisions you must follow, who has the power to promote you, and who is generally responsible for your career trajectory. When top management, be it the Board or CEO, decides cost cutting is necessary due to losses or lack of growth, you know the first decision is to cut middle management. While the real reason for your company's non-performance may be mismanagement or lack of preparedness to the rate of change, you know the first victim will be you.

Every manager stuck in the middle must manage the daily frustration of management, but it is especially aggravating in situations where you believe you have the ability to successfully resolve the issue and do it well. You know you are clear in your thinking, but you don't have the support of your bosses because there are other egos and games at play.

Your survival depends upon which organisational silo or clique you belong to, how much power you hold in that silo, how much politics you can play, and whom can you hurt to survive the cuts. Only the cunning survives, not the most accomplished! Logically, most agree the middle managers should be the leaders and decision makers, but they are hardly given any authority and so have to learn how to survive or be moved on.

How about you? You are a good worker, but you can't make yourself play politics. You are doing your job to the best of your ability. How do you avoid being victim of the cost cutting or politics? How can you grow your contribution to the company, beyond implementing the orders given from top? You may be asking how you might know what value you directly create for your company, and how you might add to it to meet the organisation's goals.

There is hope. My career was forged in all the above mentioned roles, and I survived. Over forty-seven years, I grew to become a business adviser to many businesses— and to their leaders—so that they multiplied in revenue and profitability with expanded operations. I pointed leadership to government grants and supports, and they took advantage of these opportunities to improve their companies' financial outlooks. I worked with business leaders to improve their thinking. It was greatly satisfying to see them grow and grow.

Indeed, there is a better way to manage your career, and that is to become indispensable to the organisation. You can do it without playing politics, too. In fact, you can create and contribute so much value, beyond even the existing levels, that you will transform your organisation and yourself.

You don't have to be a middle manager to learn from the lessons I share in this book. They are applicable to anyone in the organisation, whether you are the entrepreneurial owner of an SME or a startup or anyone else in management. Perhaps you had no formal training for your role. The younger generation taking over a family business, for example, may never have been trained formally, having learned on the job. Maybe you want to be respected as a professional, someone who can break the glass ceiling wielding the right knowledge. Maybe you are a female professional but not getting the recognition you deserve or get leadership roles you raise your hands for. You need to know what questions to ask, where to get the right answers, whom to trust for advice, how to manage the business finances and cash flow, survive beyond the first few years and not fail. You don't want to leave with your reputation in ruins.

It may be that you are extremely time-poor but have a dream, and the passion, to reach an aspirational goal. Do you want to become a CEO or do you simply want to feel empowered as a leader because you feel disrespected by staff and leadership? Do you have a boss who won't let go of decision making? You are in a tough position. Middle managers, I know, often have no time to study further in an MBA program or CPA or whatever. Middle managers often feel stuck at their level, typical for seconds-in-command. They are frustrated by company culture, knowing that top management is responsible. They are ready to quit.

This premise of the book is to get strong but basic steps and knowledge to you, the manager in the middle, so that you can grow and learn from my experience and exposure. I want to give you enough knowledge and know-how to improve your thinking in the face of problems. By the end, you will have learned the basics, enough to solve the problem in front of you and/or an understanding of the resources, links, books, or even specific courses that may help. This book will save you time and effort and give you the knowledge you need to handle management problems and understand what is needed to solve them, ask the right questions, and get the right answers.

This book should whet your appetite for knowledge. It does not replace an MBA or any speciality in higher studies because higher education teaches you far more. If you read this book, you will be able to understand and implement the rules, growing as a person, a professional and as a leader. You will understand what your organisation needs to grow: how to improve the financials, increase profit, reduce costs, develop a strong culture, be the cutting edge in the industry, reduce the chances of failure, and become the employer of choice.

If you don't know where to start, you can start here.

This is a small handbook for anyone seeking quick answers from someone experienced in business management, intended to improve your decision making across the whole management spectrum especially in manufacturing, operations, and supply chain. It will be most useful if viewed as a primer for a new manager or an accelerator for an existing manager feeling stuck and helpless. This book will help you:

1) ask the right questions on various subjects of daily management,
2) comprehend fully the implications of the answers you get from your team, and
3) improve the work you do based on your understanding of the answers.

This book is also for those who have spent quite a lot of time at the second and third tier of leadership, those who have good experience but lack the formal qualifications for a bachelor's or master's degree in business administration or an executive MBA.

You might say, "I have no idea about cash flow, or operations science, or long-term strategic thinking." Let me ask you a few questions: Do you understand your own household's expenditure? Then you can understand cashflow. Do you manage your family as the children grow? Then you understand management. Do you not plan for your retirement? Then you understand long-term planning? Do you not manage daily life, taking care of chores, money, time management and so on? Then you know how to respond to urgent jobs. Do you use technology every day in your home? Do you not find ways to reduce costs, reduce frustrations, improve your lifestyle? If you do all of that, then seeking a better future for your work life is just an extension. Nothing more. Section 3 of this book will help get you some science to back your management style.

The book starts with a quick reference solution table for common challenges faced by the managers. Please look for problem you are facing and then refer to rules outlined in the book's chapters as indicated.

The book is divided into four sections. The first section, UNDERSTAND & BUILD 'YOU' is to develop your practical knowledge about your own personality, what personality traits make you behave the way you do, what culture do you and can set with your management style, how much actual value add do you provide (Value add person or Non-value add person or Value creator), do you have an employee mindset or of an entrepreneur, how can you use the concept of Responsibility-Accountabilit y-Authority-Trust to improve your team and overall decision making. The second section, DEVELOP YOUR TEAM, help you do just that. The third section, INCREASE YOUR KNOWLEDGE, offers tools to equip you as you move towards excellence and grow into higher levels in the organisation or in your business. The fourth section provides a list of reference books for further reading and my conclusions on the book. Each chapter is labelled as a rule for management. I call them rules, as these became my principles to follow and contributed to the achievement of my goals. I don't call them "suggestions" because I believe that if we give ourselves the option to pick and choose learnings, we limit our abilities as effective leaders.

I hope this book helps you improve your thinking to the levels where you can grow and take right and important decisions for the company you work in. My experience of using the knowledge I have gained over life has helped me take right decisions for companies I worked for, the people I helped develop and the growth I created in advisory role I achieved in later part of my career. I am sure this book will set you on a path to learn more, achieve greater heights and mentor people to grow to their potentials.

SOLUTIONS TABLE FOR COMMON CHALLENGES FACED BY MANAGERS

Consult this table for the rules in the book that will help you address the problems that arise in management. Choose the issue from first column and open the book to the rules listed in the second column to help you in resolving that problem.

Your issue	Rule number
Becoming a value creator	1, 3, 5, 10, 20, 22
Building teams and trust	1, 6, 8, 9, 10, 11, 20
Building your dreams and goals	1, 5, 7
Business planning	5, 7, 20, 21, 22, 23
Cash flow improvements	15, 16, 17, 21, 23, 24
Changing culture and behaviours	1, 2, 6, 8, 9, 10, 11, 20
Choosing between setting up a business or accepting employment	4, 5, 7, 20, 21
Client relationship betterment	8, 21, 26, 27
Customer service improvement	6, 9, 18, 21, 25, 26
Developing your people	1, 6, 8, 9, 20, 21
Employee motivation	1, 3, 6, 8, 9, 10, 11, 20, 21

Your issue	Rule number
Evaluating opportunities	7, 20, 21, 22
Freeing up time for you	6, 7, 11, 17, 20
Accessing government support	13, 28
Growing your personality	1, 4, 10, 20, 21
Handling personality clashes	1, 4, 6, 8, 10, 11
Increasing diversity	1, 2, 3, 8, 11
Multiplying your business	3, 7, 21, 27
Profit improvement	7, 16, 19, 24
Quality improvement	17, 18, 19, 25
RAAT	6, 9, 11
Reducing costs	3, 13, 15, 16, 17, 19, 23, 24, 25
Reducing inventory	17, 19, 23, 24
Safety culture	1, 2, 17, 28
Sales growth	7, 9, 10, 19, 21, 23, 26
Setting up KPIs / Performance Management	9, 10, 15, 17, 19, 23, 24
Skill level improvement	2, 9, 11, 12
Staff engagement	1, 6, 9, 11
Understanding and managing risk	7, 14, 17, 22, 23, 27
Your value proposition	12, 20, 27

UNDERSTAND & BUILD 'YOU'

As an intelligent individual, you already know you must learn to use your strengths and work on the weaknesses to succeed. To do this, you must first understand your own personality. What are your traits? What makes you tick or boil over? Understanding who you are and how you are perceived by others is very eye-opening. You are a leader when people follow you. Your behaviour, led by your values and beliefs, will set the culture around you. Knowing your faults will help you accept what you need to change your in behaviour, whether it is the words you use, your body language, your actions or, especially, the way you direct the people following you. As a role model, what you advise people to do has to be the same as what you would do. Otherwise, you create a perception in your followers of a hypocrite. When you take time to understand your own self, the realisations you make definitely will make you a better leader and it will help you in your interactions during your work life or personal life. Once you understand yourself, you will begin to understand other people better, as well. Selling your ideas and change management becomes easy if you also can also understand the strengths and weaknesses of other people, their personality traits and background. You will improve your negotiation skills, and people will accept the changes that you propose.

RULE 1

SET YOUR PRINCIPLES AND LEAD BY EXAMPLE.

You are a leader if you are or want to become a manager. If you have one person following your directions, you are a leader. Your people will model their behaviour on you. Therefore, you as a leader need to set your principles and live by them.

The principles that direct your own actions and behaviours are generally based on your values and beliefs. Beliefs are concepts, assumptions, or ideas that we generally hold to be true, whether there is evidence or not. Beliefs come from interpretations of our religious teachings or non-religious teachings. Our values define what we deem important to us like equality, honesty, integrity, conservation of the environment, etc. Our behaviours are very much controlled by our values and beliefs. Leading with principles but not following them gives the wrong message to your people, which can cause disastrous behaviours by all and affect company culture. More on this in the next chapter.

How many times you have come across managers or owners, who always talk about integrity, honesty, and focusing on customer, but then make a quick deal on materials purchase not thinking about the customers or avoiding payment to their suppliers? What if they were avoiding the complaints about poor products or service and telling lies to customers and suppliers over product failures or shortcomings? What would you think of someone if you heard them tell you, "Don't do as I do, but do as I say?" Would you consider them a hypocrite? Someone with zero integrity? Undependable? Not credible? Definitely.

If you were described in that way as a leader in the workplace, then to what level do you think the workers around you would lower themselves to follow you?

The first rule of leadership is to be totally transparent and always live a principled life. (A good book to read on this topic is *Principle-Centered Leadership: A Leadership Model for Success* by Stephen R. Covey. I say to my children, "You should not only be honest but appear to be so. You should definitely not be dishonest but also appear not to be so." It is said that if you are always honest in your values and beliefs then you don't have to remember anything because generally you will speak and behave honestly. The people around you, your staff and colleagues, your family and especially your children, watch and learn from you. If you break the rules, especially the ones expounded by you, then they will end up with a very much exaggerated form of your worst behaviours.

There is nothing wrong in accepting your weaknesses and working hard to fix them by learning from the best in your organisation or outside, but do not attempt to cover them up or present yourself as someone else. In Rule 4 below I explain how to understand your own personality traits and behaviours as well as of others around you to become better person at understanding people. This will help how to use strengths of everyone and become a good leader, create great teams and culture.

Ask Yourself:
- ☐ What are my values and beliefs?
- ☐ Do I follow the advice I give to others myself?
- ☐ Am I 'saving a cent' instead of acting in the interest of my customers or employees?
- ☐ Do I lecture my staff on principles and slogans and then take shortcuts to nullify them?

For further study, refer to the books under Further Reading: 4, 33, 34

RULE 2

DEFINE THE CULTURE OF YOUR ORGANISATION.

The fish always rots from the head.

Ensuring a healthy culture is the biggest contribution you can make to any organisation. Culture is the foundation of a successful business yet most do not understand that the drivers and signs can be quantified and changed, if you have a good or bad culture you need to know why so you can keep it or fix it.

An organisation's culture determines its collective behaviour. It is captured in the phrase "this is how we do things around here." Culture, as taught by the Australian Institute of Company Directors in their Directorship course, is the organisation's reality, what it is like to work there, how people interact, and what behaviours are expected. The National Association of Corporate Directors, USA (www.nacdonline.org), describes it in this way: "The culture is always

- unique to every organisation
- seen in internal and external behaviours of employees at all levels
- expressed in how organisation treats their own employees

- reaches beyond the organisation in interactions with
  - customers
  - suppliers
  - community and
  - stake holders."

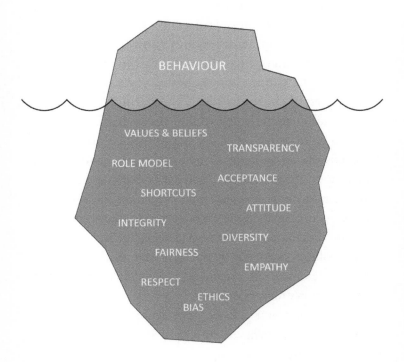

ORGANISATIONAL COLLECTIVE
BEHAVIOUR FORMATION

Image above shows, in the tip of the iceberg, the collective behaviour of an organisation, and how its people act in dealing with fellow employees, customers, suppliers, and the community every day. This behaviour comes from the values and beliefs of leadership, its biases, ethics, and attitudes, and in how leadership demonstrates integrity, transparency, acceptance of diversity in opinion, and respect for all irrespective of gender, religion, sex, background, without discrimination. These values and beliefs point to what behaviour will be considered acceptable by the top leadership. Culture is always established by top management in any organisation. To use the common adage, "the fish always rots from the head." If the culture is poor, it is a result of the values and beliefs of the leadership. The behaviours within the organisation are reflective of how the leaders behave.

As a manager, you set a positive culture if you are positive in attitude always and teach good, lawful behaviour. If you present negativity in expressions mostly and demonstrate mistrust, poor behaviour, on the other hand, you contribute to toxic cultural behaviour where employees tell lies, exhibit mistrust, engage in in-fighting and politics, turn to nepotism, and build personal power fiefdoms, all corporate actions that destroy the organisation's reputation.

Every day, you will see news reports about the way a company has behaved poorly in its dealings with its suppliers, customers or employees, and these reports point to problems within the company itself. A construction company that is not paying its suppliers demonstrates that it does not value them or their service. Likely, its practices are mirrored internally, for example in paying employees poorly for their work. When a company one day collapsed and declared bankruptcy after hiding its financial position, investigations soon revealed the owners were siphoning money out of the company to finance personal assets. It had an internal habit of creating false positioning with lies and missteps and by running away from regulatory authorities.

Examples of company cultures creating company failures are many. One of the biggest failures in the history of business was Enron Corporation, an American company which, with $101 billion in revenue (2001) and 20,000 employees working in electricity, natural gas, and communications, collapsed and was found to be using creative accounting principles. It was hiding billions of dollars of debt. Enron had assets of more than $63 billion, but it failed, taking along with it the audit company Arthur Anderson, one of the largest audit and accountancy companies, which disappeared from the corporate world. Founder Kenneth Lay and many executives were indicted, and some went to jail.

Many other examples of bad culture exist, and the leader is always found to be the perpetrator. Another example is HIH Insurance, an Australian firm led by Ray Williams. The company boasted of A$8 billion revenue, but the company collapsed owing A$5.3 billion causing tens of thousands of jobs, hold up of almost $ 2 billion of construction projects, tens of thousands insurance policy holders affected drastically with services cancelled etc. The Royal Commission report into the failure of HIH Insurance indicated various reasons but prominent were serious level of corporate mismanagement, over-priced acquisitions, too much corporate extravagance, lack of adequate provisions for insurance claims, poor commercial decisions, culture of not to question the leadership and show blind faith, risks not properly managed etc- or in other words mainly due to the "corporate culture." (Please see Parliament of Australia publication "Royal Commission into the failure of HIH Insurance Report by the Royal Commissioner the Honourable Justice Owen, April 2003 Volume I-A corporate collapse and its lessons")

Culture is set onto a harmful path when wrong behaviours are not addressed and thus permitted. It might start initially by delaying payments and using statements like "the cheque is in the mail" or "we are awaiting major payments and will pay as soon as that happens," when none of that is true. If you tell your people to lie, then they will learn to lie to you, to cheat you, and to create problems that will destroy your reputation.

How to Improve a Culture

Company culture can be improved. Having contributed to culture change at many organisations, I suggest the following steps:

1) **Understand the people and the way they feel about the company.** Asking about the issues employees face will give you so much information about what is happening. In your enquiries, use the 5 Ms suggested by the LEAN method (materials, manpower, machines, methods, and money) and ask employees about safety, communications, quality, customer service in their work areas, and then listen. In a small company, these questions can be asked in a one-on-one talk with each

employee. In a larger employee company, it can be done by survey. I have created a system called RAAT to assist with this effort, as described in Rule 6. But you will find several tools are available globally to understand the culture in your organisation.

2) **Establish and promote expectations for organisational behaviour.** Everyone must know what is expected when working with internal colleagues, external suppliers, customers, and other external people. Here, we must ensure that everyone follows basic rules. The Australian 2017 Royal Commission into Misconduct in the Banking, Superannuation and Financial Services Industry, which was carried out by Justice Hayne, according to https://www.royalcommission.gov.au/banking, acknowledged that no best practice exists for a good culture, but the following six standards need to be adhered to:

1. Obey the law.
2. Do not mislead or deceive.
3. Act fairly.
4. Provide services that are fit for purpose.
5. Deliver services with reasonable care and skill.
6. When acting for another, act in the best interest of that other.

These are the norms followed by regulatory authorities and taught everywhere as part of establishing a good corporate culture.

3) **Understand and communicate the purpose of the company.** You as a leader need to find out the purpose of the organisation. What was it set up to achieve, and what were the guiding principles for the company as set by the founders? This is also known as "the why." If there is no clarity in this, then you need to work on developing "why." This is covered later under Rule 5 where I discuss Simon Sinek. Once this is understood, you must ensure everyone relates to the guiding principles and follows them daily.

4) **Establish documented systems to monitoring and ensure the expectations are met.** The guiding principles need to be followed rigorously in all dealings internally and externally, with suppliers, customers, society, regulatory authorities, stakeholders and all the people we deal with, without exception.

5) **Engage the staff.** Staff engagement is the key to improving culture. As shown continuously through this book, I was able to change cultures previously led by autocratic control whenever I involved my staff.

6) **Review behaviour continuously.** We must live and breathe organisational expectations through our own behaviour while paying attention to the following priorities:
   - risks and compliance (appetite, matrix, review)
   - safety (WHS)
   - quality

- integrity
- rewards and punishment
- environment social governance

7) **Stay calm and create a stress-free environment for everyone in the organization.** I am not an expert at solving stress issues and can only talk about the steps that I follow:

   a) Get a creative hobby. I make pencil drawings, paintings and art whenever I can. Helps keep me quite stress free. You can look at any hobby to help your creativity- play music, construct models, DIY projects, do any thing that puts your mind away from mundane.

   b) Think positively always. Things could be worst and worrying would not help you but will create a wrong atmosphere around you.

   c) Keep moving physically. If you have a sitting job, get up and walk about every hour. This is must to stop you getting tired and have health issues.

   d) Become a member of professional body and join in meetings there to improve input into your mind, grow your social professional circle and divert you mind into meaningful and people helpful activities.

   e) Join in a charity or a not-for profit organization to volunteer. Take up a cause and involve yourself in it.

   f) Take up a physical activity – join a gym, run/walk, play golf whatever. Join yoga classes to help improve health & mindfulness.

g) Sleep well and on time in a disciplined way. Struggling to sleep can cause a lot of stress.

h) If you feel unwell, do not ignore it. Getting a medical opinion on a problem does no harm and you can resolve many issues by simple solutions. Every health problem is not a serious one but can become if ignored.

i) Remember, if you have a family, spending time with them is also crucial. Times not spent with spouse and children will be lost forever and can cause a lot of stress.

The above are by no means all the steps to be stress free. I followed these main ones to help me. You may have other steps which help. Look at organizations, books and written articles that help here as there are many.

Ask Yourself:
- ☐ Has an employee survey study been done to define the culture in your organisation?
- ☐ Is the culture of your company positive and constructive or is it survival of the most cunning?
- ☐ Do you see clear and transparent decision making in all relations and dealings with employees, customers, suppliers of your company?
- ☐ Do you get to ask or tell misguiding statements to the employees, customers, suppliers of your company? If so, have you questioned as to why?

RULE 3

KNOW YOUR ROLE. ARE YOU A VAP, NVAP OR VCP?

"If the rate of change on the outside exceeds the rate of change on the inside, the end is near" —*Jack Welch*

What do you do as a manager? Look around in your organisation at all the people. There are only three types of people in any organisation: Value Adding Persons, Non-Value Adding Persons, and Value Creating Persons.

Value Adding Person (VAP)

In each business, there are people whose roles earn direct revenue through activities which a customer pays for. These roles perform *value-add activities.*

These are the people on the floor in a factory or customer service representatives in retail or programmers writing codes or delivering product to consumers. They add value through their revenue-earning activities in their areas of operation. These employees are generally the lowest in hierarchy in any organisation. On a daily basis, they help provide the revenue that the business depends upon. Without VAPs there is no work being done, and no revenue is coming in. These employees create the products and deliver the services the company then sells to earn revenue income or sales revenue. Without them, the company cannot meet expenses or profit goals.

Non-Value Adding Person (NVAP)

The second category is people, including middle managers, who do not add direct value to the products or service provided but who are in the organisation to support the VAP. NVAPs are paid from the expenses and not paid for by the customer as the customer does not directly receive any direct benefit from NVAPs. Starting with middle managers, there are many roles created under pretext of helping to reduce the "daily firefighting load" on the senior most manager, and layers of NVAPs are added to control lower-level roles and communication, including excessive numbers put in to overcome other issues like lack of training and proper skill sets. NVAPs will be there to perform roles such as extra quality inspectors, administration staff, reception only, extra numbers of staff for any role and coordination, and mostly in layers of management between the top leadership and VAPs. For example, one type of NVAPs are those extra quality people required who identify rejects, failures, reworks, etc. If we impart extensive knowledge and provide proper tools to measure variations and quality to the actual people performing the value adding (VAP), then you will have less rejects and wastage and you don't need to put people to oversee their output quality or to check what they have done. VAP are generally good enough to learn and perform their jobs to the performance standards required and don't really need another layer to manage over them. There are some other NVAP roles you can't do without like planners

& bookkeepers, but we need to optimise the numbers. Generally, you combine purchasing and planning together and you reduce a role. And you will need one bookkeeper but they can be outsourced. In a small company I have advised, they have a bookkeeper, a part time CFO, a Board chairman with financial background which is an overkill as well as incurs high overhead costs.

All NVAPs add costs and add hardly any value to the product or service, and value is what the customer pays for. The more unnecessary NVAPs you have in your organisation, the worse the culture, politics, and overall costs. NVAPs, are let off first when costs are to be cut. If you are a NVAP, you are at risk. Do you want to stay in that zone?

Value Creating Person (VCP)

VCPs are people who will help multiply the revenue and profit. They do not cruise along with the incremental growth that happens with small efforts or small thinking. These people are the innovators, the outside-the-box thinkers, the disruptors, "Idea's executioners," the visionaries, entrepreneurs, intrapreneurs, the "Jugaad heroes." They create businesses, multiplying the growth rate, multiplying the EBIT/EBITDA/Net Profit Before Tax, and increase net assets of the business.

While other expressions above are self-explanatory, I would like to touch upon intrapreneurs. MIT Sloan School defines *intrapreneurship* as acting like an entrepreneur within an established company (https://mitsloan.mit.edu/ideas-made-to-matter/intrapreneurship-explained). It's of creating a new business or venture within an organization.

Sometimes that business becomes a new section or department or even a subsidiary spinoff. Examples of intrapreneurship (sourced from https://lmarks.com/blog/intrapreneurship-examples-to-learn-from/) include Gmail and Post-it notes. (Gmail grew out of Google's "20% time". Post-it notes came out of 3M's culture of innovation). The great companies encourage intrapreneurship and there are so many success stories across the horizon- Frito Lay- Flaming hot Cheetos, Amazon Optimum Prime, McDonald Happy meals, Sony Playstation, Sleeping Duck mattress, the list goes on.

Look around in your organisation. How many of such value creators are there? I expect that you will find only a bare few—one or two percent—who are providing such value to the business. The entrepreneur CEO will generally be in that category.

Now, would you not like to be one? You can maximise your career opportunities by following these guidelines:

- **Prioritize value-adding people or activities**: The more portion of value-adding people and activities you have in your organisation, the greater will be your ability to increase revenue, capacity, capability and to improve the bottom line. For example, don't have coordinators or team leaders or even supervisors just sitting in the office monitoring other people. Make them contribute to value adding activities. A team leader who is actually working on the line or a sales rep who is actually delivering products or a delivery person who is actually creating sales or a service coordinator who is actually providing customer service is much more useful to the business than a person sitting in an office directing people. A receptionist just greeting people when they arrive may not even have enough work – give them book keeping, invoicing or any other computer linked data work and you have a more interesting job- or best still use technology to handle your visitors thus upgrading the job.

- **Optimise non-value adding people or activities**: We need NVAPs in any organisation, but adding excessive people to take care of the confusion in channels of communication is counterproductive and adds costs, costs and costs. For example, when NVAPs are added as a layer between a top person and the VAPs, because the top leader is so busy they have no time to spend with the VAPs, it can create huge communication issues, the formation of cliques, power bases and silos.

- **Encourage and build value creators.** Make it a target to convert all VAPs and NVAPs to VCPs so your revenue and profit multiplies. The book *Jugaad Innovation: Think Frugal, Be Flexible, Generate Breakthrough Growth* by Jaideep Prabhu, Navi Radjou, and Dr. Simone Ahuja provides examples and methodology to achieve this. The intrapreneurs from within the organisation will create teams for the project, find time, within their own time if need be, and create multiplication of revenue with products, services, capacities, and capabilities. It is the responsibility of leadership to create such an atmosphere of innovation, and it can be done by following these guidelines:

o Create and encourage innovation, or *intrapreneurship*, within the business.

o Encourage people to create teams and take time to work on projects that help multiply the value addition, double the revenue or profit, multiply size by Merger & Acquisition, or create innovations to launch new technologies or products.

o Use technological advances to think ahead and get ahead of competition. Jack Welch, former Chair and CEO of General Electric, said, "If the rate of change on the outside exceeds the rate of change on the inside, the end is near."

o No value creation can happen without some stretched targets. Set up for growth. Focusing on organic growth will lead to 2% to 3% annual revenue increase. A stretched goal of 20% to 50% growth will require strategic planning and capital resources, but the results are generally tremendous.

Building value creators in your organisation should be the most important activity that you do as a leader or CEO of an SME. If you increase the number of Value Creating Persons, they can help you multiply your revenue or profit; your organisation may grow 30% to 100% in specific periods. More on how to do this will be introduced later, but remember: Staff engagement is a key to building value creators.

Ask Yourself:
- ❐ What is the number of NVAPs in your organisation? What is the percentage ratio (and yearly trends) of NVAP to VAP? What technology can be brought in to reduce NVAP?
- ❐ In your organization, do you measure revenue (a) per all persons, (b) per VAP, or (c) per NVAP?
- ❐ How many VCPs can you identify in your organisation? How many people have the potential to become VCPs?

RULE 4

SURROUND YOURSELF WITH PEOPLE WHO HAVE STRENGTHS THAT ARE YOUR WEAKNESSES.

Understanding yourself, especially your strengths and weaknesses, is very crucial to your own development and your team creation. What are your personality traits? What are the traits of the people around you? You are as good as the team you set up.

To set up a good team around you, it is essential that you surround yourself with people who have strengths that are your weaknesses. If you surround yourself with people who do not complement your strengths, you are not allowing yourself to become a good leader. If you have people around you with same strengths and personalities, it will lead to unnecessary conflicts and arguments. If you surround yourself with people who are yes-people and who have the same weaknesses and strengths as you, that is a recipe for disaster. Counter-opinion is essential for you to grow as a leader and to be effective.

It is important to understand your own personality traits and those of people around you. Personality traits determine your behaviours, responses, and reactions, generally and in crisis. The insights you gain from this analysis will tell you how to create your team, and it will help you work on your SWOT analysis, SWOT being a tabular list of Strengths, Weaknesses, Opportunities, and Threats that is useful in all setting up strategies and planning.

Whether you are leading a new business or engaging in important negotiations, you want to know the personality of the person in front of you so that you can relate to them and create a mutually amicable atmosphere to close the deal. If you can't form a relationship across the table, then the deal is going to be difficult. So, how can you, in a short time, understand the personality of the person in front of you? The best book on this subject is *Personality Plus: How to Understand Others by Understanding Yourself* by Florence Littauer. The book contains a revealing personality profile self-test that assigns a personality profile, and Littauer's insightful advice helps readers better understand themselves and others (Please see https://thepersonalities.com/). While there are a lot of personality tests as seen on https://psychologia.co/four-temperaments/, Littauer also defines personalities under four types—sanguine, phlegmatic, choleric, and melancholic—four "temperaments" based on the oldest personality types systems in the world. These four temperaments are briefly as below:

Sanguine are lively, optimistic, buoyant, and carefree. They love adventure and have high risk tolerance.

Phlegmatic personality is usually a people person. They tend to avoid conflict and always try to mediate between others to restore peace and harmony.

Choleric temperament is usually a goal-oriented person. Choleric people are very savvy, analytical, and logical. Extremely practical and straightforward, they aren't necessarily good companions or particularly friendly.

Melancholic personalities love traditions, avoid novelty and adventure, extremely thorough, serious, and accurate, they are fantastic managers with good personalities.

Most have one of the above as a major trait and then have a mix of each of above ingrained into our behaviour. The book Personality Plus will allow you to understand what type of personality and temperament you have and those of the people around you. This will then help you to interact with people accordingly. You will see that people with sanguine temperaments are good in marketing, performing arts, travel, fashion, or sports. Phlegmatic people work well in nursing, teaching, or charity. Choleric temperaments work better in taking control, management, and technology. People with melancholic temperaments do well in accounts, management, administration, and so on.

There are many tests in the world, Myers-Brigg being most popular, and you may choose any, but I found for myself, Florence Littauer's four temperaments approach is a great, simple way to master quickly the personalities you face in your career, and it helps you handle them much better, increasing your success rate on negotiations or in selling your ideas.

Now, with knowledge of your own personality and SWOT, you develop your team.

Conduct Your Own SWOT Analysis

How well do you know your strengths? I recommend the following method I have advised to many.

First, sit down and write all activities you have done in your life, in your work, at home, growing up, in your hobbies. List what you have accomplished using your personal skills, your personal interests, your creativity, and at any time during your whole life. Think starting backwards from last year, where the memory maybe sharpest and write down any activity of significance that you can remember doing, and not just at work. Write your achievements and, more importantly, write down your failures.

Go back from your childhood and go through your years in life, recording what you faced and how, the good, the bad, and the ugly. This is crucial to understanding what you are good at besides what you do in your current work role. Write it down in as much depth as you can. It will cover four to six pages, depending on how old you are. Writing in depth helps you understand all you done and where you have shown strength of character, or skill or knowledge in decision making, and out of where your experience grew.

Once written, from here you will be able to see your strengths and weaknesses, what you really do like to do, what your passion seems to be, and what you are not good at and should avoid. Then you will know how you want to use your strengths and avoid your weaknesses.

This is the work you need to do before you decide to whether you are ready to move into an entrepreneurial kind of a role where you run your own business or if you should remain an employee. (See Rule 5 for more on that.)

In my advisory role, someone referred a QA Manager to ring me for advice on his career as he wanted a change. He was doing well in his job, but something was gnawing at him from inside to aim for higher and better roles. I asked him to do a personal SWOT analysis instead of just looking at changing jobs or going to a different company. He was surprised when I asked him to do that but felt good about attempting it. Once he did this exercise, he understood he was good at and passionate about fixing musical instruments and had even developed a patentable product. While he had it in him, he had no one to guide him on how to launch a product. I told him to continue in his current job, since he was far more comfortable with employment than entrepreneurship, and on the side, develop the patent to launch it as a product. He stopped looking for a new job but started working on setting up a business based on the patentable product.

Here I must discuss mental strength or toughness. According to Lyn Christian (https://www.linkedin. com/in/lynchristian/) quoting Journal of Applied Sport Psychology research by Graham Jones, Sheldon Hanton, Declan Connaughton (https://doi. org/10.1080/10413200290103509), mental toughness means possessing a psychological edge that enables you to cope up with demands, perform consistently and remain determined, focused & confident under pressure. The research identified 12 attributes that elite athletes follow to stay tough mentally to cope with failures, anxiety etc and continue to motivate themselves to stay ahead. This is all the more important when you are feeling down and can take wrong decisions. When you are down, it is the worst period to take important decisions in life. So develop mental toughness to overcome such weak moments.

Ask Yourself:
- ☐ Have you done the personality test indicated and found out what personality traits you have- sanguine, phlegmatic, choleric or melancholic?
- ☐ Are you able to look at behavior of people around you and connect the personality traits information to describe what their strengths and weaknesses are?
- ☐ Would you attempt a confidential personal SWOT analysis to really understand better your own successes and failure reasons?

For further study, please see books 4 and 6 on the resources list under Further Reading.

RULE 5

KNOW YOUR BUSINESS MINDSET. ARE YOU AN ENTREPRENEUR OR AN EMPLOYEE?

"If you have the dream, the passion and the discipline, you can conquer the world."

How many people have a dream or desire to set up their own business as an entrepreneur and moving on from their job as a manager in the middle? This especially happens as a midlife-crisis decision as frustrations come up in life or in your job or you have a sudden realisation of time passing.

So many people have come to me to ask for assistance with setting up their own business. "I want to make lots of money," they say. "Please give me some advice." But they don't understand the work involved in setting up their own business, or their own entitlement mentality around employment benefits, like a monthly salary, a nine-to-five schedule, paid leave, fringe benefits provided etc. Before you decide which world is best for you, it is important to understand your mindset.

Do you have an employee mentality or an entrepreneur's?

Let us understand the definition of *entrepreneurship* first: Entrepreneurship is the process of designing, launching, and running a new business, and offering a product, process or service for sale or hire. If you want to start your own business, you need to have passion: Entrepreneurship always starts with a passion or dream which becomes an obsession. You must know your "why." I recommend watching Simon Sinek's TEDx talk, "How Great Leaders Inspire Action." In it, he underlines the importance of knowing your "why" — you need to communicate your belief in what you do. Sinek points out that inspirational leaders of innovative companies not only tell others what they do or how they do it, they tell others *why* they believe in it. If you are considering going into business, you need to really look into yourself to decide if you have the right mental attitude or not.

You must also understand whether you have an employee mentality or a business mentality. Think:

1) Are you prepared for an initial lack of regular income and perks until your business starts to give you what you are looking for?

2) Are you (and your family) in the comfort zone with a monthly paycheck and a nine-to-five schedule? Are you comfortable being part of the organisation's hierarchy, doing what your bosses advise or guide you to do?

If you answer yes to the question in Number 2, you have an employee mindset. As an entrepreneur, you need to consider that your role will ask you to work 24/7 and be disciplined in your thinking. You will own it all—the successes, the failures, assets, and liabilities.

Robert Kiyosaki, the author of *Rich Dad Poor Dad*, says, "Money is just an idea," and "Money is not the goal. Money has no value. The value comes from the dreams money helps achieve." Going into business is a marathon not a sprint; you want to create wealth, not quick money.

To be an entrepreneur, you must keep these points in mind:

- **Entrepreneurship asks you to take risks.** What risk profile do you have? What age are you? Your risk profile is conditioned by what stage of life you are in. If you are young, risks can and will be possible, but as you move to older age or closer to retirement, then lower risk factors become more important because low risk is crucial to your future life.
- **Entrepreneurship asks you to become clear about your values and beliefs**, *values* being the things that we deem important and *beliefs* what we feel to be true.
- **To be an entrepreneur, you must have access to resources.** The 5Ms describe it best: money, materials, machines, methods, and manpower (that is, human capital).
- The matrix below explains the relation of passion and resources.

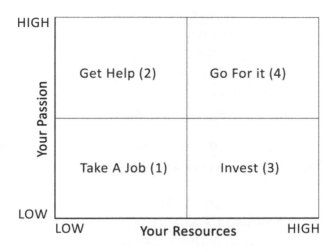

PASSION AND RESOURCES MATRIX

Depending on where you see yourself in the Passion and Resources Matrix, there are actions you can take to grow your opportunities.

Take a Job (1) – If you have low passion and low resources—become an employee first but, you can:

- Get a dream: Get dream and passion for some goals. Set goals and get some achievements under your belt and a purpose in life. Learning to dream comes from creating a visual of what you want for yourself, your family, your mental satisfaction, and so on.
- Develop resources: Set a goal for saving money, budgeting, etc. Develop a passive income (for example – with Network Marketing like Amway)

to increase your financial base. You could delve into share market if you understand that it is for the long term and do it with professional advice. You could also acquire further qualifications in your field of interest. Increasing your strengths will help you uplift your resources.

Get Help (2) – When your passion to a cause or goal is high, but you lack resources then you can:

- <u>Learn to dream</u>: Follow the suggestions described above under Take a Job (1).
- <u>Get Support</u>: Turn to external sources to increase your financial skills. Set a deposit for security to arrange bank support or find an investor who will help you. Your passion for the project, presented correctly, will excite others too. It is a difficult task, but flying through hoops is essential for you to achieve your goals. If you are eligible, you will be entitled to government support; many governments, especially in western world, provide a lot of support.

Invest (3) – Investing is your main action when passion is low, but resources are high. Try these strategies:

- <u>Partner</u>: Get a partner or find a business to invest in or buy blue chip and other shares. But analyse options using appropriate professionals' institutes/ organisations for advice, follow their advice and invest wisely!
- <u>Invest</u>: Decide what is the focus. If it is side income, then real estate is a good option and

blue chip shares, if you prefer. If it is to set up a business, look for opportunities (see Rule 7 for more details). Learn about innovating and how to see the gaps in market. Look at new technology, new materials, industry trends, government announcements on policies and investments incentives by them etc. Match them to your strengths and not follow blindly what every one seems to be doing. Get a mentor to guide you and help set you up (See Rule 10). Be careful when you choose your mentor; look for someone with the correct attitude to mentor you. You can also get merger and acquisitions experts to help you. Proper due diligence in the business is essential before your decision for your investment. Research the company, technology, sectors, leadership of the business, and potential of the business before you invest. Proper contracts and registration with government are needed to before you can take ownership so be prepared for spends on lawyers.

Go for It (4) – When you have both passion and resources, the sky is the limit, but your first step is to seriously consider the idea you want to build your business upon. Move forward with careful consideration:

- <u>Build on your idea</u>: What do you want to build your wealth around? Read the book "Rich Dad Poor Dad" by Robert Kiyosaki. To enter an industry, first get a job in that to understand the intricacies, problems and solutions and the risks involved. Get some knowledge on the financials (see Rule 14) and prepare a Business Plan (See Rules 27).

- <u>Practice discipline</u>: Becoming financially wise, using time wisely and being frugal will help you in the start-up.
- <u>Be prepared for 24/7</u>: Business is not a 9-to-5 role. Period. Understand that you will, in the beginning, struggle with time and resources as you set up your business, and it could be stressful.
- <u>Play on your strengths</u>: It is crucial you use your strengths and know your limitations. You are not God and cannot do everything.
- <u>Set up a strong business foundation</u>: Your business structure is crucial to your success. Believe in profit maximisation and not just tax minimisation. Follow expert advice from your accountant, mentor and the industry practice. Think 3 to 5 years ahead.
- <u>Use professionals</u>: Accept the help of professionals to do the roles that you can't do or should not need to do. Roles like payroll, bookkeeping, HR, and legal are best done by qualified professionals. Saving cents does not save dollars: it can cause legal compliance issues that you don't need.

I fell in love with manufacturing operations, as to me it creates value addition with physical products and related services that solve problems for the consumers.

Ask Yourself:

☐ Do you have a dream that keeps you awake at night that you want to achieve?

☐ Are you ready for the sacrifices that come with setting on your own business. That is, can you accept "the price to pay"?

☐ Are you prepared to learn and be a follower of the leaders in the same game before you try to be a leader? (Don't reinvent the wheel.)

☐ What risk profile do you have – do you think like an entitled employee or an entrepreneur?

For further study, please see books list under Further Reading: 1, 32,

RULE 6

MASTER THE RAAT CONCEPT: RESPONSIBILITY, ACCOUNTABILITY, AUTHORITY AND TRUST

As a manager, every day your people implement directions given by you, and then you keep a tab on what is going on under your watch. But have you ever thought that people under you, who look up to you, could themselves help you achieve a lot more than what you get currently through them? I want to introduce the concept of *Responsibility, Accountability, Authority and Trust* to help you achieve a lot more from your people.

"John" runs a baking products factory and controls every decision in the business. Everyone is always waiting for all decisions to be made, as that is what John wants. John has a team of people making the bakery products (value-adding activities) as well as administration, coordination, and supervision (non-value adding roles) to meet the daily customer service requirements, but John dictates every decision, every day. John is in firefighting mode, spending all his hours "managing" the people, resources, and urgent customer issues. The business has plateaued at a level that John feels he can control, and so it is hardly growing and almost stagnant. John can't let go of control, despite my regular advice. I see this scenario every day in businesses I have worked with, and the same causes are always the problem:

- John is working *in* the business not *on* it, which means he is spending too much time inside day-to-day operations and not working on growing the business, or looking at future where the business can go. He does not trust his team of people to perform their roles, and he can't let go of micromanaging it. As a result, the business is not realising its potential.
- No next-level leadership has been developed to take over. If John falls sick, it is difficult to manage; the team depends too much for any decision on John.

At this stage, the business is not exit-ready as the decision making is not done by the team, only by John. The business runs totally as "John dependent" and not as an organisation.

The solution lies in collaborative workplaces where the people work and deliver their own selves as *self-managed teams*. To understand this concept and how to make this happen we need to understand the three concepts of Responsibility, Accountability, and Authority, which leads to Trust (RAAT©). I have refined this concept based on my thoughts and experience, but acknowledge the definitions also provided by Vedantu.com at https://www.vedantu.com/commerce/authority-responsibility-and-accountabilityedantu and other places.

Responsibility

The best definition of responsibility is "that it is the ownership of a task." Being responsible means delivering the task within the parameters of time, costs, and performance, to the levels of acceptance of the stakeholders. In business, ownership of a task may be someone operating a machine in a line producing a product, or a driver making the delivery of what a customer has ordered, or a retail salesperson serving the customer and making the actual sale. These are the most basic of tasks and without them no work will be ever completed. People are asked to be responsible for their tasks, and the completed tasks realise the revenue for the company.

Accountability

The United Nations Economic and Social Commission for Western Asia defines accountability as answerability, liability, and the expectation of account-giving to someone over your actions. You may be the cog in the wheel, but how important are you in the whole scheme of organisation? Do you have any idea? How does your output or work create value or contribute to the profits (and costs) of the organisation? You may be responsible for a task, but you and your boss are accountable for the overall outcome that the task leads to. For example, the quantity and quality of the whole line output for the day creates revenue, costs, and profits for the day as measured by Overall Equipment Effectiveness (OEE; see Rule 17 under KPIs. Please also see books under Further Reading at the end).

Authority

The *Oxford Dictionary* defines authority as "the power or right to give orders, make decisions, and enforce obedience." Others like Shiksha Online define it as the right or power assigned to achieve certain organisational objectives.

In day-to-day operations, decision making needs to be delegated to the team leaders or staff members, with an escalation clause to lay out limits. For example, staff can be given the authority to make purchasing decisions; the quality department can be allowed to determine release date of the product manufactured for the customer; employees can be handed the authority to stop the line or operations because the quality of output does not seem right; or, teams leaders can arrange / hire more staff when the need arises. Usually, all these decisions mean direct spending or costs and, generally, they are not allowed; every such decision must be countersigned or made only by the managers themselves. I see from my experience the authority to make decisions is the least allowed, and management is reluctant to let go of this decision making but granting this authority allows the team's leadership to be developed.

Trust

The dictionary *Merriam-Webster* provides the best definition of trust as "assured reliance on the character, ability, strength or truth of someone or something" and "one in which confidence is placed." When we provide the people below us to take Responsibility, Accountability and Authority, we show them our Trust. We trust them to do right by the organisation. Once we convince our people that we do trust them with the decisions they take for the company, they will begin to trust us back. Trust is always mutual; trust cannot be one-sided. One cannot have long-lasting trust if there is no mutual relationship and openness and transparency in decision making, and allowing lower-level staff to make decisions, under your mentorship, lets them make mistakes and learn from them, which helps them continue to improve.

The relationship between responsibility, accountability, and authority also defines the culture of the organisation. How the top, middle, and lower management levels perform in each component of RAA will determine the T and, so, the culture.

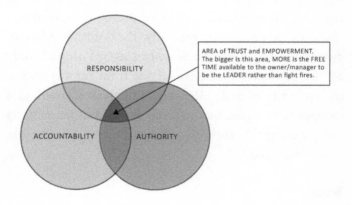

RAAT- PERFECT TEMPLATE

The above Venn diagram is a visual presentation of the concept, and the size of each circle represents the level/intensity of each of the three. The Area of Trust and

Empowerment will be best when each circle is of equal size. This is very important to understand. Unequal size is a problem, as we see in the explanation below for VAPs, NVAPs and VCPs.

In the typical hierarchy of an organisation, we give VAPs full responsibility, a bit of accountability, and very little authority for decision making, and as a result there a need for layers of management to manage the VAPs. For VAPs, normally, the RAAT diagram looks like the one depicted below. There is lots of responsibility, hardly any accountability, and very low authority.

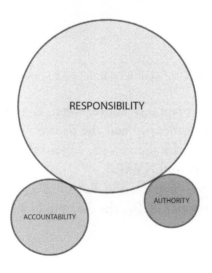

RAAT of VALUE ADDING PERSONS- TYPICALLY.

For NVAPs, the diagram generally looks like this, with lots of authority, some accountability, and low responsibility.

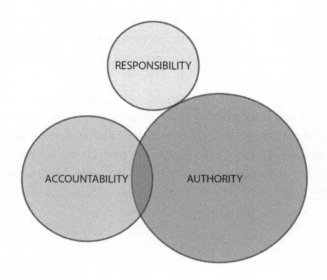

RAAT of NON VALUE ADDING PERSONS -TYPICALLY

In both diagrams above, what is the trust level between the leadership and the people following them? When you see the above, what actions do you expect to see from VAPs and NVAPs?

When we consider the RAAT diagram for Value Creating Persons (VCPs), the diagram looks like this:

RAAT of VALUE CREATING PERSONS.

VCPs take on the full responsibility, accountability and authority as they are drivers and visionaries to undertake the growth that takes the organisations into high achievement areas, multiplying revenue and profits.

Responsibility *without* accountability, or accountability *without* responsibility, or authority *without* any responsibility or accountability are risky situations to even contemplate. You can see the catastrophe is coming. There are so many examples of scandals in Australia and across the world that show this vividly, in companies in all industries, like banking, airline, financial, retail, sports, and government. You can probably see that also in your organisation. When a boss only gives responsibility, but does not communicate any accountability and authority, what do the people do? They don't use their own thinking, they just do what they are told, they go home, then they repeat this pattern the next day, forever. The solution lies in you. You must create teams of people to whom you can give responsibility, accountability and authority, all three.

I encourage you now to complete an exercise. Apply the RAAT concept to the people you see around you or in the news. Identify the RAAT diagram for each and consider the value of their professions. For example, what does the diagram look like for a bureaucrat? A politician? The chairperson of a company? Are there roles VAPs, NVAPs, or VCPs?

Use the RAAT Tool to Improve Your Culture

I have developed RAAT as a tool for top management to understand how each component is being achieved, to identify gaps, and on which one specifically they need to concentrate to fix organisational issues.

The **RAAT** tool is a set of questions for both the employees and the management separately. Each question reflects the status of each element from the viewpoint of employees and the management individually separately, thereby giving us perspective. In computation of results, we can see the gap in perspective within the responses to every question put forth between the employees and the management. The questions are linked to issues seen in any organisation and responses reflect the shortcomings in specific areas of Quality, People & Team Work, Skill & Knowledge Development, Technology & Tools Provision, Performance & Productivity, Costs Budgets & Profitability, Purpose, and Strategy & Risks. The data collected is confidential and is not traceable to sources for the organisation, thus maintaining sanctity. Only the report will be sent over to the organisation with specific areas of action needed. Details of the RAAT Test are being provided on my website www.managersinthemiddle.com.

RULE 7

IMPROVE YOUR
DECISION MAKING.

How as a manager you can take more authority? By proving yourself through:

- big picture thinking
- improving profitability for long-term and not just short-term
- reducing costs to improve profitability
- eliminating firefighting habits where you must control everything yourself
- engaging with staff, and
- showing the improvements in the culture in the organisation

Decision making is a crucial part of authority. To help you grow as a leader, you must learn to make the right decisions. Below are some pointers and tools to help you improve your decision making.

Taking and Giving Authority (Delegating)

Every day in your life you are making decisions in all types of situations. Your decision making is normally conditioned by the amount of risk associated with the result in terms of financial loss, risk of reputation, of trust with people, etc. How do you fare?

Let me explain with the example of TopNotch Quality Foods (TNQF; name fictionalised to maintain privacy), formed and run by "Alex." TNQF produces various products like confectionary, health bars products etc. in a plant set up about ten years ago. Alex was wasting a lot of time placing orders and making payments even for consumables and small items that really did not need his decision making, because he did not trust and wanted to keep control. He took the advice of a mentor to set up delegation of spending authority to the next layer of his leadership team based on how much financial risk was involved. The delegation rules were set up based on types of expenses and the items. Any capital equipment purchase was delegated to the team leadership in the plant if it was already in the budget. If not, the decision went to Alex. Daily expenses for consumables were limited to $500; anything above that limit went to Alex for approval. The financial risks determined the delegation. For decisions of smaller financial risk, the decision making is easier as the loss is more acceptable. However, the larger the risks to the finances, productivity etc., the lower the decision-making authority.

Use an Escalation Clause: Allow your staff to take on responsibility and authority showing accountability at lower risk levels. Then, raise the decision making for higher risk levels and increased financial outlay. Until then, everyone must understand when to escalate a decision to their manager. Escalation of decision making means you delegate decisions to those below you on the hierarchy up to a certain financial amount. You can help everyone understand when to escalate by using the Delegation Matrix. This is a good way to manage risk. The matrix below can help you in deciding where and how to delegate powers.

DELEGATION MATRIX

Risk Taking

What is your risk taking profile? What is your organisation's tolerance of risk? Every company that I have worked in or advised were found to not really understand the concept of risk.

All decisions are fraught with risk. Risk is present in every strategic plan you make, any decision to launch a new product, in any capacity expansion plans, in hiring decisions, new product designs, or in any advertising or investment decisions. Plans do not always work out the way they were envisioned. Your decisions, then, must be considered based on the *likelihood* of things going right or wrong and the *impact* of the decision, or the cost to the company. When you consider the likelihood of loss, how much loss will the company allow? You must understand in a very basic way the risk profile of your company leadership.

Use a risk matrix: Every day you make decisions based on what your risk profile, but you may not be aware of the science of risk measurement, which can assist you in decision making. I like to promote the use of the Risk Matrix in your decision making. The 5x5 matrix below, as provided by ISO 31000*, shows the relationship between the likelihood of a decision or action or incident and the impact levels that the same can cause. Depending upon your industry, "likelihood" and "impact" can be assigned various levels. The vertical column on extreme left describes the likelihood of an incident or decision on a scale from Very Likely to Very Unlikely; the top horizontal row shows a scale measuring level of impact from Negligible to Severe. The relation of each Likelihood and Impact level describes the risk. Colours are used to assist with interpretation; Use red areas to indicate high risk decisions, yellow for medium risks, while green areas will show low risks. Decisions can be evaluated based on what type of industry you work in (hospitals and airlines will have different risk profiles as compared to, say, an office) and so risk assessment and decision making will change.

Likelihood	Impact				
	Negligible (1)	Minor (2)	Moderate (3)	Significant (4)	Severe (5)
Very Likely (5)	Low Med (5)	Medium (10)	Med Hi (15)	High (20)	High (25)
Likely (4)	Low (4)	Low Med (8)	Medium (12)	Med Hi (16)	High (20)
Possible (3)	Low (3)	Low Med (6)	Medium (9)	Med Hi (12)	Med Hi (15)
Unlikely (2)	Low (2)	Low Med (4)	Low Med (6)	Medium (8)	Med Hi (10)
Very Unlikely (1)	Low (1)	Low (2)	Low Med (3)	Medium (4)	Medium (5)

RISK MATRIX

The above matrix is useful decision-making tool, especially once the *context* is established. The *context* of a buyer is different from a seller, so each will prepare the matrix differently. For example, a liability risk matrix will be different from the airline's point of view when compared to that of a passenger. Once you have established the context you can score Likelihood and Impact and so create a multiplied number for each risk. If we give a score of 1 to 5 for each level of Likelihood and Impact, 1 being least likely or impactful and 5 being most, then a Moderate Impact and Possible Likelihood will give a score of 9, whereas Severe Impact and Very Likely will score 25. The decision making then becomes easy for the risks identified.

Explaining this with an example will help. If your company is deciding to launch a new product, then we need to ensure we have done a market study and competitor analysis before launching. Once that is done, then the likelihood of failure will be Unlikely while the impact will still be Significant, giving us a risk rating of Medium, or a score of 16. However, if not enough market analysis and study has been done and the product is being launched in a rush, then the likelihood of failure will be Very Likely and the impact will Severe, giving us a risk rating of High, or a score of 25. The decision of launching or not launching will become clearer with this risk analysis.

Footnote: *The Risk Matrix above comes from ISO 31000's Risk Management guidelines, which are available at https://www.iso.org/iso-31000-risk-management.html. The guidelines provide principles, a framework, and a process for managing risk. It can be used by any organization regardless of its size, activity, or sector. There are now software also becoming available for risks & compliance – an example is at https://lahebo.com/.

Evaluating Opportunities

You will come across opportunities daily and you will need to make a decision to pursue them or not. When I am presented with an opportunity, there are some rules that I follow:

- Always look at the opportunity on a long-term basis.
- Short-term opportunities generally earn quick money, but do not take into account the actual costs of disruption to your daily business, as your costings may not account for the time you spent on the short-term benefit.
- Opportunities need to be considered strategically and not haphazardly or on ad-hoc basis.
- Spend time testing the assumptions and analysing risks with your team before you take on the opportunity.
- What will it really cost to deliver the outcomes?

The best method to evaluate these opportunities is by using a Benefit-Effort matrix (based the Ease-Value Matrix invented by Espen Sivertsen, the CEO of Ivaldi), as below:

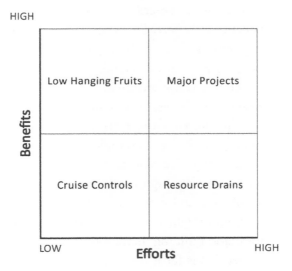

BENEFITS–EFFORTS MATRIX

The matrix above explains the relationship between benefits and effort, and you can analyse an opportunity from the context and point-of-view of your organization. *Benefits* are as measured by revenue and net profits, capacity utilisation, time savings, cost reductions, elimination of frustrations, etc. *Effort* is measured by the 5Ms, money, machines, manpower/human capital, methods and materials.

Notes:

1) *Low-hanging fruit* describes such opportunities which, as per your analysis, will require low effort and costs as compared to the promised benefits in revenue and profitability.

2) *Cruise control* describes an opportunity low in benefits and effort. This will be when the changes required are low; if the capability and capacity exist, then go ahead and take them on. But never say no to any opportunity.

3) *Resource drain* describes an opportunity with low benefits but which may require a lot of effort to implement. A classic example is an order to supply from a large size reputable customer group that does not allow high profit margins and takes a lot of time and money to make the sale; in this case, you might pursue the order if you need it for brand building, better buyer relations, or the strategy calls for it under a much bigger picture game. Otherwise, resist doing this.

4) *Major projects* help you reach the outcomes that are very much needed for your company. Even though the efforts are high, so are the benefits. Value creation projects or intrapreneurship projects will come under this category as they will involve a lot of resources for team effort, planning, and execution. Setting up a new plant, exploring export markets, or expanding facilities into a new geographical location are some examples. The benefits of multiplied revenue, increased net profits, and expansion into new markets can be life-changing for the business and so these projects need effort to be executed well.

Setting Goals

One of the best practices is to set proper goals and targets and then establish plans to achieve them. Your decision making becomes clear and focused if you have a target to achieve. The longer-term the target is, the better it is for your consistency in decision making and for your long-term future. Jim Dornan, a leader and mentor I followed till he passed away, quoting Lewis Carroll, would say: "If you don't know where you are going, any road will take you there." What he meant was this: if you don't set a direction for your future, you are doing nothing more than setting cruise control and travelling to wherever your circumstances will take you.

When you search for "how to set goals," you will find advice about SMART goals. This acronym describes goals in this way:

> Specific, Measurable, Achievable, Relevant/ Realistic and Time-bound

SMART is a good way to start the discipline of goal setting and achievement.

Now, does setting any goal really make meaningful change in your life or career? If you simply set up targets and goals that are based on easy picking or normal effort, you are not going to achieve any transformational change in your life. I don't agree fully with setting *just* SMART goals as it basically wants you to set nominally achievable goals; SMART goals do not ask you to push yourself or stretch yourself and your resources so that you really make a difference. You want to multiply sales and/or profits, not increase them by an annual three -four percent.

I believe any goals we set must stretch us. <u>The goals must be aspirational</u>. That is, they must represent what we aspire to achieve rather than what we can achieve with some effort. Goals must stretch our efforts and require us to work hard to achieve them. Those goals that really make us sweat more than normal are transformational. They will multiply growth and profits and truly change the business or our work and give us a real sense of achievement.

Every year, a company can set a growth target of just above CPI growth level or benchmark to the industry they are in. That is a SMART goal, but will it change the company's market share or profits? Asking all employees to ensure customer service levels are maintained is a SMART goal, but does it increase the customer base drastically and so allow value creation? On the other hand, setting a goal to double the revenue in three to five years gives the business a target of 20% growth annually. That will really stretch a company's resources and people, but the company now doubles its size in five years!

Aspirational goals are always set for long-term periods like three to five years. Once you have a five-year goal, all your decisions can be directed towards achieving that single goal, and the whole organisation works towards as well. Setting a one-year goal annually does provide you a SMART goal, but the company is not going to double its size and, hence, it cannot be a Value Creating Goal.

I always ask my clients "Where do you want to see yourself in five years?" We then work on achieving that goal by working backwards, divide the goal into chunks over the next five years, then setting plans for each year according to the five-year goal. Try that approach and you will see where you can take the company!

Ask Yourself:

- ☐ Are you a big-picture (future) thinker or do you have a micro-mindset focused on the short term?
- ☐ What is your risk profile: Are you a risk taker or risk avoider? Are you a calculated risk taker or reckless risk taker?
- ☐ Do you trust people enough to let go and delegate decision making, or do you micromanage your people?
- ☐ What kind of goal-setting exercise do you believe in? What is an aspirational five-year goal for you?

If you want to read more on this topic, consult the Further Reading list, referring to 1, 4, 7, 8, 9, 10.

SECTION 2

DEVELOPING YOUR TEAM

As a leader, you can't do it all alone and you need a team to achieve organisational goals. With people following you, you need to understand the strengths first and then use the collective strength of the whole team to achieve what you want to, whether you are working with a team you created or not. While you develop yourself in your career journey, you also need to understand how to build a team and take it to excellence. This section of the book will help you create high-achieving teams as well as create the next level of leadership to free you up to go where you aspire. This section will show you how to almost clone yourself, which sustains your philosophy so you are proud of the organization you create.

RULE 8

UNDERSTAND IQ, EQ, AND CQ

All the people you meet and interact with may not have the IQ, EQ and CQ that you have. What are these concepts?

IQ

Everyone knows Intelligence Quotient (IQ) as a tool used to understand the intelligence level of a person. The higher the IQ, the more intelligent the person is supposed to be. In practice, IQ is normally tested with people who know mainly English/Western World languages as almost all tests are designed to reflect IQ in these languages only. That does not mean people who think in other languages and dialects are not at a reasonable level of IQ. We need to remember that people with stronger language skills in English/Western World languages will test better, and people who do not understand English will score worse. Many people I have worked with from non-English speaking, were extremely intelligent and have enriched my life. Further, many intellectually challenged people, or so-called "disabled" people, can be great workers for specific tasks with good training. So, using an IQ test to classify a person is a great injustice to them and to you.

EI or EQ

Your Emotional Intelligence (EI) or Emotional Quotient (EQ) reflects how you behave with others as a leader. The term, which has been in existence for a long time now, was made popular by Danial Goleman in his book Working with *Emotional Intelligence*. EQ or EI is accepted as a way to identify skills and characteristics that drive leadership performance. It is generally seen that people with higher emotional intelligence have better mental health, job performance and leadership skills.

An assessment of person's levels of EQ or EI indicates how someone behaves in everyday life, how they will perform tasks and solve emotional problems without their own subjectiveness. The Mayer-Salovey-Caruso Emotional Intelligence Test (MSCEIT) asks respondents to identify emotions expressed in the face, interpret feelings, predict how people will react, and describe how their decisions and emotions integrate. To learn more about the MSCEIT, see https://langleygroup.com.au/msceit-assessment/. You can also consult one of the best books on this topic by Fritz Shoemaker, *ChEQmate: Using Corporate Held Emotional Intelligence as a Winning Business Strategy*.

CQ

Cultural Quotient (CQ) is seen as a measure of capability to relate to and work across different cultures and geographically diverse areas. This is a recent phenomenon coined in 2002 by P. Christopher Earley and has become important with increased global interaction in business, government, and academia.

How well you deal with people across different cultures has a lot of bearing on how you will expand your sphere of activities and how much respect you can earn across the world. You need to understand the cultures and behaviours of the people across the world and respect their way of life and actions. Learning the cultures of others and their diversity will help increase the success rate of your interactions.

Examples of poor CQ behaviour, which can cause considerable complaints, are:

- words expressing racism
- comments on people's religions, skin colour, languages, traditions
- lack of awareness about specific lifestyle issues (e.g., offering alcohol or pork to a Muslim, offering beef to a Hindu, using white/black envelopes to give gifts to people of Chinese descent, etc.).

There are many cultural issues that can arise to affect your relationships; some transgressions will break the law if you are not careful.

Ask Yourself:
- ☐ Do you try to understand the reason for the behaviour of a person of other descent or culture?
- ☐ Do people exhibit fear around you or are they able to freely communicate with you?
- ☐ How often do you ever try to empathise with or adapt to or accommodate the other person?

RULE 9

DEVELOP YOUR PEOPLE.

*People always want to grow mentally
and develop themselves.*

No business can grow or survive with just one person – the owner or the manager. Everyone needs a team of people to help them carry out various roles within the organisation. The more professional you are in developing your people, the better your organisation will be and the lighter the load on you.

Improving the skill level of your employees is your paramount responsibility; it increases accountability, and employees take on authority, leading to a positive work culture, as described in Rule 6. People never refuse training or skill upliftment or professional development. That is my experience.

Development means growth for everyone in the business, for you, your superior, your subordinates. It has two components:

1. Skill upliftment for every one in the business or organisation to increase Value Addition and Value Creation including driving innovation
2. Professional development of the individual to become a Value Creator (see Rule 3)

How To Prioritize Skill Development

Establish a training policy and display it. Let me explain by a joke everyone has heard. A CFO goes to the CEO and says, "Why are we encouraging training and spending money on that? What if they leave after the training?" The CEO replies, "What if we don't train them and they stay? Where would that leave us?" A flat joke with a serious message.

Do you even have a training policy? As an SME or an organisation looking to survive, do you have a separate training policy document displayed in the organisation like you display the Quality Policy or OH&S Policy? You may ask, "Why do I need a training policy? I am all for training, and I always encourage training and development for everyone in our organisation." This is a common response to a question like this. It is full of intent but there is no defined action.

Let me now ask you a few questions regarding your business. Answer "Yes" or "No" as you read through them.

1) Do you have a training budget based on training needs? Y/N
2) Does every employee go through a minimum of one training every year? Y/N
3) Do you have a strategic document listing the skills and knowledge requirements of your business for the next 3 to 5 years? Y/N
4) Do you have a documented second- and third-tier leadership development plan? Y/N
5) Do you have a professional development programme for your leadership team? Y/N

If you answered "No" to any of the above questions, then you have a training issue facing your organisation and you are not ready for the future. That is a very strong statement to make, really? Let us review this a bit.

Do you have a clear understanding of Value Adding Persons, Non-Value Adding Persons and Value Creators in your organisation? Each of these people are different, but there is only one path for growth and that is Value Creation. See Rule 3 above.

Use a skills matrix. A skills matrix is a great way to set up a development plan for everyone in the organisation. Preparing a skills matrix is a simple way to present a development plan for every person in the organisation, from directors to the workers. It requires creating a worksheet with the names of each person in the organisation listed in the rows, and the skill sets, professional skills, specialist skills listed in the columns. The illustration besides shows a skills matrix.

SKILL MATRIX

SKILL LEVELS	B=Beginner	S=Skilled	T=Trainer

Name Of Employee	Equipment / Process A						Supply chain OTHER Y/N							Sales & Marketing			AICD
	Change Overs	Startup/ Shutdown	Operate	Pack	Documents	Cleanup	Trouble Shoot	Warehouse	First Aid	Maintenance	QC Checks	Forklift	Pallet Wrap	Label Machines	Prospecting	Networking		Director Graduate Ship
A	S	S	S	S	B	S	B	N	Y	N	Y	N						
B																		
Sales															T	S		
DIRECTOR																		B

The Skill Matrix has top rows indicating the skills required, going into depth and details to perform the roles. The column on left has the names of all employees from leadership to bottom most layer of hierarchy. Each skill held by the employee is marked in the appropriate cell with symbols like B= Beginner, S = Skilled, T = Trainer, Y= yes, N = No to indicate the level of skillset, clearly indicating the improvements needed and aimed for continuous growth. This Skill Matrix is displayed openly in the organisation and the annual performance wage increase and bonuses are based on this.

This also is linked to the path of the business, so we define the training needs for the people to that path, and then define the timeline and programme for training. In your organisation you may further we need to add other skills as below:

Skills: Advance skills, EQ/ CQ for leadership development etc.

Knowledge: Business category subjects like financials, OEE, Digital technologies, Risk Matrix, Office365/IT systems, Robotics AI etc

Once you have the skills matrix in place, we must look at the execution of the training.

Find time to develop and train your employees. Many times, I hear questions like "When do we find time to train, we are so busy?" My counter question always has been "What do you do with employees when there is a breakdown or when they are unable to do their roles for some reason and suddenly have free time? Do you send them home?" My personal policy always was this: Anytime a person is free from doing their job, then they go and train under someone. I allowed no confusion on this. When the skills matrix is displayed openly and people know their professional development plan, their next skill level, then they will themselves ask, "Can I learn this now, as per the Skill Matrix, since I have some free time now?"

Align the development programme with salary and wages. Link the skills matrix to salary and wages and show that multiskilled or higher skilled people and people with expertise are recognised with higher salaries, wages, and benefits. Once you declare this in the Training Policy, people will begin asking for training. When we don't display the skills matrix to show the evidence of skill levels openly, it leaves to interpretation the benefits given to people, causing unnecessary strife within the workforce.

Ask Yourself:
- ☐ Do you have a documented Training Policy covering every employee for both Professional and Personal development?
- ☐ Do you give training a priority for activities when people become available free from doing their work- due to breakdowns, shortage of materials/labour etc?
- ☐ Do you followup and execute plans with all regarding their development needs?

RULE 10

UNDERSTAND THE POWER OF A MENTOR.

Is training only for staff? What about you, the SME owner, or the middle manager? Do you understand the concept and power of mentorship? Do you have a mentor to go to when you need to bounce around ideas? Getting a mentor is one of the greatest steps you will take in developing yourself and in building your organisation.

Who is mentor? I like this definition from an article by Matt D'Angelo in *Business News Daily* https://www.businessnewsdaily.com/6248-how-to-find-mentor.html) "Mentorship is a mutually beneficial professional relationship in which an experienced individual (the mentor) imparts knowledge, expertise and wisdom to a less experienced person (the mentee) while simultaneously honing their mentoring skills. An effective mentor can guide the mentee professionally while maintaining a friendly and supportive relationship. A mentor should always have the mentee's best interests in mind and tailor their mentorship style to meet their needs."

A mentor generally is a person who has achieved success in their field, someone who people generally look up to with respect and get inspiration. The role of the mentor is not to undertake any actions or work, but to help develop mentee to take better decisions.

In normal circumstances, a mentee will run a scenario past the mentor and ask the mentor if the decisions they are taking are right. The mentor's most common answer in these discussions will typically be prefaced with the phrase "Have you considered…?" The reason for this is simple: Your mentor is there to help you grow as a leader. As the adage says, "If you give someone a fish, you have fed them for a day. Teach them how to fish, and you have fed them for life." Your mentor guides you to think for yourself and advises you whether you are on the correct path or not.

How to choose your mentor?

Your mentor should be:

- someone you respect
- a known authority on the subject in which you need to be mentored
- available and agreeable to mentor you for a period of years
- someone who can give you time on a monthly basis
- willing to give you full responsibility for organising the meeting, keeping notes, and documenting action plans
- guiding you in your work, not taking it on themselves to do it for you

It is up to you to find the person to mentor you. Look at yourself and consult your SWOT (Rule 4) to understand what weaknesses you need help with. Find a high achiever in your field of activity and approach them to ask if they will mentor you. Don't be afraid to ask the person who inspires you in your industry. Approach them. The worst they might say is no. What if they say yes?

You may need more than one mentor. That decision will be based on the fields that you work in. For example, in your middle manager role, you might need a career-building mentor and another one to focus on a skillset that you lack. Say you are a middle manager in food manufacturing. You might like to approach a business leader in that industry (a chairperson or a company director, for example) and another one from within your organisation in the subject of finance, let's say. Do not get multiple mentors for the same area of improvement, as you will get confused. Choose your mentors carefully. As you attain new levels in your organisation, you might need a mentor at a higher level to guide you.

Expose yourself to leadership training. Follow thought leaders to develop your knowledge. Some examples of great thinkers whose books can help you grow professionally are Simon Sinek, Steve Jobs, Jack Welch. Consult the book resources list under Further Reading to see my recommended titles. When you become a director, you will also need to understand your legal and the regulatory responsibilities. Do you know which ones to follow? A training course with the Institute of Company Directors in your country will provide good exposure and awareness (see www.aicd.com.au or https://www.nacdonline.org/ or https://www.iod.com/ or any other organization in your country.

Ask Yourself:

- ☐ Do you have any thought leader in your industry you would like to be mentored by?
- ☐ Are there any mentoring programmes being run by professional bodies you can join in?
- ☐ Do you follow any of global leaders on their Instagram or Linkedin etc?

CREATE SELF-MANAGED TEAMS.

Engage with your people.

I come to a very important question. Do you really understand your people? Every day, we have people managing others. How do you think the people who are being managed feel about it?

Haven't you heard these comments often?

- "I wish our boss left the job to us to do instead of micromanaging us."
- "Our manager really should spend some time with us to know how we do these jobs."
- "Does the manager even understand what we can do?"

Let us look at the lives of the people who report to you. These people work with you only eight hours a day. In the remaining sixteen hours, what do they do? Each of these people runs their own life outside of the workplace. They manage their own personal affairs and their household finances, care for their children and dependents, and improve their status. Is there any reason they can't manage their area of work? Is it necessary to put a NVAP manager in the middle place to manage the people, especially the VAPs? Is there a way to let your own people, the VAPs, run their own small area of operations without you micromanaging them?

We can train people to understand their roles in the business, and we can train them to self-manage. The way to engage with the people is to involve them in sharing the responsibility, understanding accountability, and allowing them to take on authority.

Operating by creating structured teams is a great way to improve culture, increase engagement and really reduce inefficiencies in the manufacturing and operations (and in fact any where in any organisations). The various ways to create teams can be shown in the image below:

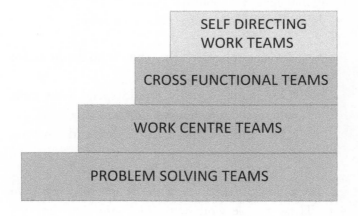

FORMING TEAMS

The various teams are explained below:

a. Problem Solving Teams are created to solve a particular problem or issue and may comprise small group of people.

b. Work Centre Teams comprise all members working on a work centre or line including people working in all shifts on the work centre including engineering personnel.

c. Cross Functional Teams are formed by people from all departments across the subject which may involve different locations, functions and levels. An actual example in a large multinational organisation I advised, was to create a "Supply Chain Effectiveness Improvement Team" for a complex long gestation product supply process across various countries. It involved all people from planning, inventory, purchasing, logistics, manufacturing, customer service working with a LEAN implantation expert etc to analyse the problem and issues and create an improved supply chain of reduced cycle time, inventory levels, ease in planning time and lower supply failure risks.

d. Self-Managed Teams or also called self-directed teams operate independently on an area or process centre taking all decisions of the section like daily operations, arranging people, servicing customer orders, overtimes, sharing people/roles, training, continuous improvement etc. Here the leadership lets them achieve the goals set jointly by them with the organisation's leadership. This is the ultimate in staff engagement.

Further explanation follows after the examples below.

At many different organisations, I restructured personnel into self-managed teams. At one place, as an engineer, I created the first ever problem-solving team for a large work centre producing about 200 pieces per minute. The products were perennially on back-order (meaning the customers were always waiting for supplies), but we could never meet the demand due to equipment malperformance. To address this problem, we formed a team of all the people working on the work centre, including the two shift operations and maintenance staff and held structured weekly meeting with minutes, action points given to all team members and reviewed every week. The team met every week on a fixed day and time come rain, hail or shine. The team managed the work centre operations. After six months, we had removed the backorder and converted the whole work centre line into a highly effective and productive work centre. The success of this first team led to the formation of five more teams in that plant with regular meeting once a week for each team. This team structure was spread across to the other three plants on the large site. A separate Total Productive Maintenance (TPM) team of the maintenance team was created to run the engineering and maintenance.

Another successful restructuring took place by me at another site where very high percentage of the workers were either injured and at home or working only partially. The plant was running at a loss. When I arrived at the manufacturing unit, I saw the culture was very toxic and staff morale was down in the pits. A large proportion of the workforce was on Workcover, an insurance driven programme to support workers who could not work due to workplace injury, and the insurance premium was costing the company $90,000 annually (around in 1996-97). The injury rate was affecting morale and the output performance, resulting in a loss-making unit. The managing director asked me to improve the culture and convert the unit to profit.

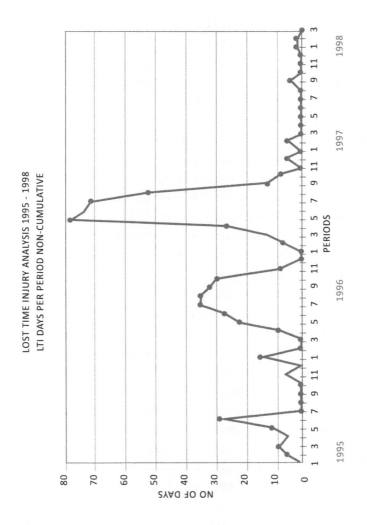

ACTUAL WORKPLACE INJURIES TRANSFORMATION

Working with the HR person, I restructured the whole site into teams, convinced people from the floor-level, VAPs (see Rule 3), to become team leaders, and mentored them. We introduced team meetings and implemented the principles of RAAT (see Rule 6), giving team leaders the accountability and authority to make day-to-day decisions in collaboration with teammates. The operations were then taken over by the team leaders under my guidance. This freed up time for me to grow the business by taking on more work and better utilising the assets. I also worked with each of the injured workers and brought them back on site with a dedicated return-to-work programme, and we fixed all the equipment issues that were contributing to injuries and fatigue.

As a result of the move from an autocratic style of management to team management, the culture changed. Over nine months, morale improved, and the injury-causing facilities were removed; the plant became a profit-making venture within 1.25 years. These efforts resulted in an immediate drop in injuries on a sustained basis, and the reduced injury rate was maintained at almost zero incidents over the next few years, leading to almost nil Lost Time Injury (LTI) and, consequently, saving hundreds of thousands in insurance premiums (the annual premium was reduced from \$90,000 to \$10,000). This has been one of my life's most important achievements: increasing safety, reducing injuries and insurance premiums. This transformation is evident in the graph besides, where you see the extreme values and fluctuations in lost time between January 1995 to Oct 1997 and a smooth nil or single digit incident thereafter Nov 1997 onwards, all because of structuring into teams who were operating the whole plant mostly by themselves.

I have many more examples, and many more are documented in books, like Maverick by Ricardo Semmler, on self-managed and self-directed teams. Essentially, the Industrial Age is giving way to The Participation Age where employees are participating in the decision making and sharing in ownership of the decisions. Would you rather create silos in your organisation, or create teams that work towards a common goal without controlling by people over people? Lots of public and private organisations are discovering this and taking advantage of it. Techniques are available to assist.

So how do you develop teams that you can trust and empower? When I formed my first team, as explained above, I was asked, "What are you talking about? Teams? We all work as a team here." Ask yourself this: Is working together called a team? To me, a *team* is created when we build a structure to work together, with rules. There is an immediate difference when a team is formed formally:

- The team runs meetings and identifies solutions.
- The team sets objectives and goals.
- Authority and responsibility are shared, and accountability taken on board.
- Ideas are generated, discussed, and actioned.

Steps to Team Success
a) <u>Form the teams</u>: Structuring into teams as in image "Forming Teams" and explanation below there.
b) <u>Identify team participants:</u> Everyone involved with the area of work will be part of the team.

This is crucial for complete engagement. A team always needs a Moderator or a facilitator to help the team perform especially in the beginning.

c) <u>Set the objectives of the team</u>: Set the goals and objectives based on the purpose of the team. The team decides the actual goal based on company objectives and goals.

d) <u>Hold team meetings</u>: It is essential that every team meets on a regular basis. As a manager, you see meetings happen all the time in leadership because the discussions create decisions. So, that will be the goal of any team in their own meetings. Here are guidelines to follow in team meetings:

   i. Fix the day and time of the meeting. The meeting time must never, repeat never, be changed or postponed.

   ii. The meetings should be held weekly/fortnightly as per the designated day and time.

   iii. If there are two or three shifts, then the meetings will be held combining two shifts together and one shift alone on a rotating basis. One week, day shift and afternoon shift will meet together and night shift will meet alone; the following week, day shift and night shift will meet together and afternoon shift will meet alone; and so on.

   iv. The schedule for all the meetings is issued for the whole year.

e) <u>Set ground rules for the team meetings:</u> The following are the ground rules of the team meetings:

   i. All team members will meet at the scheduled meeting time, free from their work. The line should be shut down, because full concentration is essential for all team members.

ii. The team will choose the following three roles:

1) *Chairperson* – The position of chairperson will be rotating, and everyone will hold this position by turn.

2) *Timekeeper* – The timekeeper will ensure the meeting does not last more than one hour. They also ensure the discussion stays relevant to the team's objectives.

3) *Minute Taker* – The minute taker will write down the discussion and record who is responsible for follow-up actions.

iii. All team members will be allowed to have a say in the discussions. Most team discussions are hijacked by overpowering voices, and this is not to be allowed.

iv. Everyone's opinion is as important as another's, so meeting decorum must be followed.

v. Team discussions will not involve any other matter except the laid-out objective of the team. No company policies, no personal issues, or politics and gossip will be permitted to divert attention from the objective. Any issue that concerns company policy will be passed on to the leadership team, and that's it.

f) <u>The team champion will be the facilitator</u>: This person is generally outside the team from leadership/ management and their main actions will be: a) to help conduct the meeting in such a way as to bring out contribution from all; b) to ensure completion of and to help work on the actions assigned to team members; and c) to help in any matter that affects the performance of the team.

g) Have fun and <u>develop a team motto</u>: Team members should have key words and phrases at the back of their minds to guide decisions and actions, such as:

- What we make, we make with pride.
- We make what the customer wants.
- Zero chances = Zero accidents.
- Make everyone's life easy.
- Remove everyday frustrations.
- Not necessarily faster but smarter.
- Defect-free.
- We are it — the buck stops with the team.

Training Your Teams

A team meeting will not result in anything useful if company leadership does not give the team freedom to be responsible/accountable/authorised for their area of work. The success of a team is best guaranteed when there is total commitment, involvement, and support of the owner or senior manager. This commitment from management contributes to a culture that allows to people take on responsibility with accountability and authority—it asks workers to own their roles and to make decisions.

Self-managed teams are also good places for leadership development. In your business, create teams with all who are involved on the process lines or in work sections in particular locations (like in retail). Select team leaders from these teams. You will make it clear to the team leaders that they will continue to add value and not suddenly become a boss, but you will provide training to them, improve their skills, and mentor them to take decisions with delegation limits, and show them how to escalate decisions that are not within their limits. Communicate daily with the team leaders. This creates a sense of trust within and empowerment of the people, who then participate in growing the business. This is not new science and has been happening for quite some time.

There are various other techniques like in LEAN (see Rule 19) and Total Employee Involvement (TEI – see https://cmoe.com/) where the organisation get transformed totally by staff engagement. There are now a lot of companies using the staff engagement processes and techniques to transform their organisations.

To make good decisions, teams need to understand problem-solving, and there are various techniques and tools that the team must be trained upon, for example:

- Cause and Effect Diagram: This tool helps the team understand that the problem is best solved at the cause end and not the effect end. Also known as Fish Bone Diagram, it helps a team really drill down to the causes of any problem, which can then be tackled one by one in priority.

- <u>5 Whys</u>: This is a technique used to get to the root cause of the problem, not just the immediate reason. The technique works because if we ask why every time, we start looking at the problem and keep asking why to each answer, ultimately we will land at the real reason. In practice, it looks like this:

  We missed the delivery today.
  Why?
  The product was not ready.
  Why?
  The packing machine broke down as usual.
  Why?
  We do not have a preventive maintenance programme to keep it running well.
  Why?
  We lost our fitter and have not recruited anyone else to save costs.
  So our cost saving idea has cost us a customer delivery miss. Fix the real cause and you will fix the consequence of the issue.

Improving Communication Across the Organisation

In my work at-least over a hundred organisations, poor communication is the biggest issue. People complain about lack of information on what is happening in the company and there are normally no avenues for discussion and sharing of information in real time. Poor communication causes confusion, and people cannot perform their roles when important information is lost in the channels of communication. This problem is compounded by silo cultures, typical in larger organisations.

I have found the best way to keep everyone in the loop is to use Visual Communication Boards as communication centres. An example of the Visual Communication Board is shown besides. Drawn on a white board, it is hung in a common pathway of the organisation so everyone passes it by often. This Visual Communication Board becomes the centre of all communications. Every day, team leaders can hold their short daily meeting in front of this board and team members can update each other on what happened yesterday, what is happening today, and any issues related to people, safety, quality, etc.

The board contains the vision, strategic plan, upcoming events, as well as performance graphs on safety, OEE, and other key performance indicators (KPIs). It also is a place for communication exchange on daily issues that are being faced. Under Issues to handle, the rules of communication can be written, as below:

Rules: 1) Anyone can write the issue, in just a word or two. 2) When handled, it is ticked by the person responding and completing the task. 3) Removal only by the person who wrote it, to keep the sanctity of the board, or by the manager." Various versions of the Visual Communication Board exist in many companies and it is an important tool to improve communication across the various departments.

WEEKLY PLANS & SCHEDULES	CORPORATE MISSION STATEMENTS, STRATEGIC PLAN & TARGETS ETC.	KEY PERFORMANCES

KEY PERFORMANCES: OEE, Accidents, Downtime, Scrap %, DIFOT, Overtime

ISSUES TO HANDLE

Rules: 1) Anyone can write the issue, in just a word or two. 2) When handled it is ticked by person responding & completing the task. 3) Removal only by the person who wrote it to keep the sanctity Or the anager

DEPARTMENT/ LINE	QUALITY ISSUES	MATERIAL ISSUES	SAFETY ISSUES	PRODUCTION	PACKING	WAREHOUSE	ENGINEERING
AREA 1							
Work Centre 1		Item needed by dd/mm					
Work Centre 2	Wrong colour						
Shed							Leaking water
OFFICE							
Etc.							

VISUAL COMMUNICATION BOARD

Ask Yourself:

☐ What formal teams or team structure do you have in your organisation?

☐ Do you have formal team meetings on a regular basis with minute-taking and actions delegated to team members for their areas of work?

☐ When did you last attend a formally structured team meeting?

For more knowledge see books under 5, 15, 20.27, 33

INCREASE YOUR BUSINESS KNOWLEDGE

As you understand you and develop your team, you need to be able to guide your team to operate effectively and grow the organisation. This section is built around increasing your own knowledge of various management science concepts and tools that will assist in improving your thinking so that you can lead the team/section you operate in and help multiply revenue, profitability, and effectiveness in the organisation. This section will give you inputs to change the direction you are headed towards for the best outcome for yourself as a leader and for the organization. There are many courses also available to get further expertise on subjects that I touch. Understanding the value of a mentor, that can provide decades of knowledge in a compressed time frame, can fast track your career.

RULE 12

BECOME THE SUBJECT KNOWLEDGE EXPERT.

Knowledge empowers, and in-depth knowledge provides excellence.

How many times have I met people, in companies including in start-ups, who have a lot of passion but don't have any depth of knowledge in their subject area? These people then go looking for outside experts, sometimes for most basic work. Let me explain with an actual example that I handled.

A start-up entrepreneur developed a specific food product, but he did not fully understand the techniques behind manufacturing of the same. He had hardly any money but was ready to sacrifice his own salary to hire a consultant to solve the issues. I asked him to put a hold on everything and, instead, spend time researching to build his knowledge on the product, ingredients, technologies available and to try to collect from different sources most answers himself. After some time, he contacted me and thanked me. Not only had his research saved him money, but it had also increased his subject expertise tremendously. He no longer had to be dependent upon others, which was going to cost as well as could have also handed over control of his innovation to others.

In your role in the company you work in, you may be aware that you lack in-depth knowledge of the products and services, but still you don't spend time to become expert enough to train people, handle all the issues, or improve product and services. Generally, all trainings provided by companies to supervisors and managers focus on management—how to manage people better, resolve their conflicts, and maybe comply to rules and regulations— and so we tend to become experts only in how to manage others (also called *leadership qualities* in HR jargon) and our depth of knowledge in other areas, like products, remains shallow.

Why do we look at one part of our role (managing people) and leave other parts (management sciences and operational effectiveness) to outsiders? Examples like this are so common:

- *"I don't know anything about accounts. I will let my accountant answer that."*
- *"In my role, I can only focus on one thing at a time, not on everything."*
- *"I don't have an idea of what to do in this subject and also have no time, so I will hire a consultant or find someone to help me do it."*
- *"I am an idea person. I don't get into details too much and leave it to the experts."*

What is stopping you from learning in depth the subject of the job or business you are in, so that you can handle the questions and the risks yourself?

One of my clients was a small business just getting started. It was quoted $5,000 for the preparation of a cash flow budget. Of course, the owner could not afford it and so came to me. I advised her by giving her a free template and helping her fill out the details in the worksheet. One week later, we had a cash flow budget for the next year, which she had prepared herself, and so she was able to manage the cash flow herself.

How to Find Knowledge and Trusted Sources

Whichever subject, trade, or type of business you are in, you must become the most knowledgeable person in that. Don't depend upon others to feed you information that you cannot check or test yourself; determine if the information being provided is wrong or misplaced.

These days, locating information is not difficult at all. Learn to search for subjects on the internet. It is the accuracy of the information that is a problem. Searching will give you options. Google has become a universal source of information due to the algorithm they developed. There are other search engines, too, like Microsoft Bing, Yahoo, etc. Now AI (Artificial Intelligence) has introduced so many options. But remember the GIGO principle- Garbage In Garbage Out. So, if the information on internet is wrong, your search feedback will be useless. Your trust in the results partly depends on the subject matter you are searching for, so you need to search using multiple sources to get a balance of information. Just don't click on the first link you see: it most probably will be a sponsored link (placed on top by the search engine for position against payment), so it may or may not be the best source. Learn to identify the best sources of data, too, and with practice you will get better at finding accurate information in books, webpages, podcasts, and authored papers. I have found that following sources generally provide higher levels of credible and truthful information:

- industry associations and professional membership bodies- Become a member to access information,
- government links, for legal/legislations, regulatory and country information,
- academia, established universities and colleges, subject-matter authorities, emeritus professors
- peer-approved books, articles, and published research.

Please be careful while reading from company publications, news articles, and individually published articles as they may be biased and need to be analysed with competitive sources to get a balance.

Leaders are Readers. The more knowledge you gain, the less you will pay for experts, and the more you will be able to ask the right questions.

Ask Yourself:
- ☐ What kind of books do I read?
- ☐ What resources do I have access to through which I can increase my subject knowledge? Are they based in recognized best practices?
- ☐ Am I a member of professional membership bodies in my field or other related subjects? Do I attend the activities or courses offered by those associations?

RULE 13

FIND SUPPORT AND GRANTS AVAILABLE FROM GOVERNMENT AGENCIES.

Every government is keen to show support to its industry. All governments at federal, state, or local levels, in every government anywhere in the world, always have industry or economic development or investment support and professionals appointed to support business. Every government also provides policy and guidelines for the businesses to grow. These policy and guidelines vary between federal, state, and local government levels and depend upon the focus and the strategic initiatives of the government department. They are supported by government funding initiatives, and normally offer funding with co-contribution by the business.

The main activities of the professional support available are intended to:

- provide guidance on the government policy, guidelines, and funding available,
- assist the various government levels to meet their political, financial, legal, and economic announcements,

- guide the businesses through coordination within various governmental departments to resolve issues they face, e.g., land tax, planning, health, food safety, OHS, etc.
- help file applications for projects under the funding and grants announced by the government,
- gain concessions, if possible, for the various tax, duties, etc., to support business growth.

It is important that a business connects with government at all levels to find the supports, fundings, grants and assistances available in whatever they need. It is also important a business stays in touch with the concerned departments to know what policy decisions are happening that can then support the business.

The assistance is also available to improve innovations and exports in many governments. There are support available to claim Research & Development expenses and export market development etc. Most government departments these are focussing on sustainability and environment and any industry that wants to reduce wastage. Find out more from the appropriate government department looking after these supports.

There are specific methods, eligibility, and requirements for each application to the grants and funds announced. These applications are normally announced publicly and opened for a short period. Businesses can submit applications for projects as per the eligibility guidelines using a specific application template. All grant applications require a business plan, proven financial viability, a budget, and require that the project meet the grant's merit criteria. In my work, I have helped bring millions of dollars to clients who applied for specific criteria-based equipment expansion projects, which successfully increased their capacities, allowing them to launch many new products, multiply their revenue (not just grow marginally), and increase profits. Many examples exist of the businesses I helped like a pasta manufacturer, in a few years, expanded from a small plant and almost quadrupled its capacity and factory size, with revenue increasing almost six times. Another company has, over the years, received over $700,000 in grants and other support from government and was able to multiply its capacity and product revenue.

Applications can be made by the business itself (the preferred method) or by using private agents who help file with some costs. The best way to get proper assistance is to involve the government department's personnel, who can help you complete the applications before filing them. They are quite happy to help too.

DON'T BE SCARED
OF FINANCIALS.

"They are actually easy to understand and
very useful for your decision making and
monitoring the health of your business."

When asked about any aspect of financials, most managers, SME businesses owners, or corporate professionals will tell me, "I don't know, but I have accountants who will know." The accountants seem to control the finances without letting others know too much. The scariest part of the business data for everyone seems to be the financials—everyone who is not an accountant.

How many people have drawn a blank when asked about what their EBIT is or EBITDA, or Accounts Receivables or Accounts Payables? They don't seem to understand that the organisation's effectiveness, cash flow management, inventory control, or day-to-day working capital requirements depend upon just a handful of financials.

Please note this section cannot replace an accounting course as all financials must meet international standards established by each country's regulatory departments. (See the note below for more information.) Accountants are qualified and trained to comply with tax and financial regulations to present the true and fair accounts. Your role as manager is to know the financial implications of your daily decisions. This rule and section will allow you to glean, from the various reports your accountants prepare, the trends and issues facing your company.

If you are a director of the company, you have to sign off on all annual financials declaring the numbers to be a fair and true picture of the company's business, and that becomes your legal liability. Each annual report contains many pearls of data that show what is happening and point to trends within the organisation, which are the result of the decisions made on a daily basis. Every manager must know how their day-to-day decisions can contribute to financial issues, cash flow problems, bad debts, costs, money blocked in inventories, etc. The financials reports themselves are not scary, and once you understand which data to use and how, the numbers will become your best friends, helping you run your area of the business which you may be responsible for as a manager. I am sharing this mainly to give you just enough basics to analyse and understand the financial trends (upwards or downwards) that are happening in the most fundamental numbers to keep track of and which will help run and manage the business. If you want to really go deeper, then off course, you must join in an accountancy course.

All you need to really know is that there are three main accounting statements. These are the Profit and Loss Statement or Report, the Balance Sheet Statement, and the Statement of Cash Flow. All three statements are explained below. They will give you information that will tell you what makes or breaks the business.

1. **Profit and Loss Statement or Report**

- Your business's purpose is to generate revenue through the sale of products or services to customers. **Revenue** is the income generated by your business.
- You incur **Expenses**, or costs, in the creation of the products or services you provide.
- Revenue or income must cover the expenses and costs incurred.
  - If the revenue is greater than all the costs incurred, you have **Profit**.
  - If the revenue is less than all the costs incurred, you have **Loss**.

Basically, the Profit and Loss statement is presented to show the following:

REVENUE minus COSTS & EXPENSES = PROFIT/LOSS

PROFIT minus INCOME TAX = NET PROFIT AFTER TAX

2. **Balance Sheet Statement**

In this process of earning revenue, the business creates assets and liabilities.

- **Assets** are defined as "what you own." Assets are items like inventory stock, equipment, amounts receivable from customers, cash in the bank, etc.
- **Liabilities** are defined as "what you owe to others." Liabilities can be the amounts you owe

to suppliers, banks, tax department, shareholders, others, etc.

- The difference between Assets and Liabilities gives us the **Net Assets** or **Equity**.

This explains, in a very simplistic way, what is reflected in a Balance Sheet. So, a Balance Sheet reflects:

ASSETS minus LIABILITIES = NET ASSETS or EQUITY

3. **Statement of Cash Flows:**

The Statement of Cash Flows describes the net cash flow from the various financial transactions carried out during the financial year by the business in its operating, investing, and financing activities. It measures the **Net Change in Cash Flow** at the end of the financial year after all actual transfers of receipts, payments, borrowings, taxes, dividends, etc., are accounted for, showing the net cash outflow as positive or negative. The statement provides a health check on the business and crucial numbers to ensure positive net operating cash flow, sufficient generation and self-generating business and test of solvency, etc.

Please see the table below as a summary of each of the Financial Statements.

Types of Financial Statements

Financial Statement	Main Purpose
Profit and Loss Statement or Report	Provides statement of EARNINGS or REVENUES, EXPENSES and resultant PROFITS or LOSS REVENUE – COSTS & EXPENSES = PROFIT/LOSS
Balance Sheet	Provides statement of ASSETS (what you own), LIABILITIES (what you owe to others) and NET ASSETS. ASSETS – LIABILITIES = NET ASSETS or EQUITY
Statement of Cash Flows	Provides the NET CHANGE IN CASH FLOW as the business spends and receives cash due to: • OPERATING ACTIVITIES (e.g., Payables and Receivables) • INVESTING ACTIVITIES (e.g. Equipment), and • FINANCING ACTIVITIES (e.g. dividends, borrowings etc).

These basic top-level financials of your company provide a lot of information and are essential to help your decision making. If you just plot the graphs to see the trends year by year basis as to what is happening to them, you will see if you are managing your financials well or not. Going deeper into each item named above will provide deeper level of information to know what to fix.

These are expressed in terms of simple ratios which are the be-all of decision making and explained further in next rule.

Please look at your country's tax compliance regime to understand the templates of each of the above three statements. The rules to be followed by all globally are explained in note below.

Note: all financials and accounts in almost every country should only be prepared as per the International Financial Reporting Standards (IFRS). Each country adopts basic principles to design the standards and formats that business must follow. These are prepared by certified accountants under the Chartered Professional Accounting (CPA) or Chartered Accounting (CA) associations. For your country's standards, please see https://www.ifrs.org/ and websites of the respective CPA or CA Association or tax department.

All companies and businesses entities are required to submit these Financials Statements annually to each country's respective Tax Office. These are reflected in the currency of the respective country and signed by company directors or authorised representatives. Compliance to each country's tax standards is a legal requirement, and non-compliance is punishable with fines, imprisonment, bans on company directorship, etc.

RULE 15

MASTER THE USE OF THE FINANCIAL INFORMATION.

We need to make a sense of all these financial data prepared by the accounts to help us take the right decisions for the company. These data are not so useful if you see them simply as once a year numbers in a table. Therefore, all three financial statements (see Rule 14 above for details) will always provide at least two years of data.

But our interest is to look for the trends across the years as they are reported, so check the numbers for basic trends. Are they going up or down? For example, we need to understand if revenue is going up or down, costs are trending up or down, profits up or down, assets up or down, liabilities up or down etc.

The Importance of Ratios

Absolute numbers going up or down do not, I repeat *do not*, by themselves provide any meaningful information until they are calculated as a ratio. (Please see Rule 17 on key performance indicators to understand this more.) For example, if sales in 2020 was $5 million and in 2021 is $6 million, then there is a clear increase. But if the costs are mentioned as $4 million and $5 million, respectively, the comparison of these cost numbers of $5 million against $4 million has no meaning as we do not know if actually the costs went up or down *unless* we can compare it as percentage of revenue by carrying out the ratio of costs to revenue for each respective year. Calculating this ratio in the example is shown in the table below:

Percentage of Revenue Calculation

	2020	2021
Costs / Revenue, %	$4M / $5M = 80%	$5M / $6M = 83.3%

This percentage (%) is a ratio, which clearly shows that the costs were higher as compared to revenue in 2021 when measured against 2020. So, we must calculate same ratios to compare year on year trends to know how we are performing.

Now, What Is a Ratio?

The definition of *ratio* is "a value relative to another."

In financial ratios we always compare a financial number relative to another number, and that is generally to the number representing the sales revenue generated. Benchmarking becomes easy if we compare every business's cost, profits, etc. in percentage of revenue generated. We can compare any department, industry, country, or sector if we use this calculation. However, there are many other ratios we need to look at to understand our day-to-day performance, which I share below.

To measure performance, monitor these ratios year over year to see the trends in your business. This will help you understand what is happening and where you are heading.

Important and Crucial but Simple Financial Ratios

We will look at the simple ratios that make or break the business. By knowing these ratios to calculate, you will be able to see:

- where the business is headed
- your cost of goods sold (COGS)
- problems like lack of cash flow and how to manage it
- the overheads and how they are affecting the costing of the products
- the profit margins you are making
- how to stay in control of your bank loan repayments and capital investments
- how to maximise the profit and minimise the tax payable.

If you know these ratios, you can set up financial KPIs throughout the organisation, which you can monitor on a regular basis rather than depend upon the formal reporting from your accountant, which may take a few days, weeks, or months to be compiled.

Out of the many financial ratios to consider, the most important to understand are just a few as those shown below. They may look a lot, but I have a list of 125 ratios that I can choose from, as required, for each business that I advise. Further description is supplied in the paragraphs below to help you understand the importance that you should give to each. You will need to look at some of these only when specific decisions need to be made, like for capital investment, strategy, mergers and acquisitions. If you monitor the following ratios, you cannot go wrong. These will keep your business in strong daily profit maximisation and growth mode. Ask your accounts people to give you these monthly.

Key Financial Ratios for Business Monitoring

Ratio	Description ("/" below means divided by)	This Year	Last Year	Trends should be as below
EBIT as a %	Earnings Before Interest & Tax (EBIT) / Revenue			Upwards
EBITDA as a %	Earnings Before Interest, Tax Depreciation & Amortisation (EBITDA) / Revenue			Upwards
Debtor Days (=Accounts Receivables), Days	(Trade Debtors / Revenue) X 365			Less than 50 days
Stock Days (money stuck in Inventory), Days	(Stock / Cost of Goods) X 365			Around 30 days
Creditor Days (Accounts Payables), Days	(Trade Creditors / Purchases) X 365			Less than 60 days
Value Add, %	(Revenue – Cost of bought in materials and services) / Revenue			60%–80%
Revenue Growth, %	[(Current Revenue – Previous Year Revenue) / Previous Year Revenue]			Upwards
Gross Profit, %	(Gross Profit / Revenue)			Upwards

Overheads (excluding interest), %	(Overheads or Operating Expenses / Revenue)			Downwards
Net Profit After Tax, %	(Net Profit After Tax / Revenue)			Upwards
Working Capital, %	(Working Capital, i.e. Current Assets–Current Liabilities) / Revenue			15%
Current Ratio	Current Assets / Current Liabilities			1.5
Quick Ratio	(Current Assets – Stock) / Current Liabilities			1.0
Asset Turnover, Ratio	Revenue/Total Assets			3 to 5
Return on Total Assets, %	EBIT / Total Assets			12%–17%
Debt to Equity, Ratio	Total Debt / Equity			0.6–2.0
Leverage, Ratio	Total Liabilities / Equity			0.5–2.0
Salaries and Wages, %	(Total Salaries & Wages) / Revenue			20%–30%
Sales per Full Time Employee (FTE), $	Revenue / Number of FTE			Monitor Targets

While most ratios are quite clear by definition, there are a few which may need further explanation, which are described below:

EBIT and EBITDA

EBIT (Earnings Before Interest and Taxes) and EBITDA (Earnings Before Interest, Taxes, Depreciation and Amortisation) are two simple terms that a manager needs to understand to use in their effort to create real value. The example in the table below shows how to calculate EBIT, or Operating Profit. It is one most important ratio for any business.

EBIT, or Operating Profit Calculation example

Sales Revenue	$100,000
Total Cost of Goods Sold (CoGS)	$45,000
COGS as % Sales	45.0%
Gross Profit	$55,000
Gross Margin as % of Sales (GP / Sales)	55.0%
Operating Expenses (Overheads):	
Total Operating Expenses	$45,000.00
Operating expenses as % of Sales	45%
Operating Profit (EBIT)	$10,000.00
EBIT as % of Sales	10%

EBIT, or Net Profit Before Tax, comes from Gross Margins minus the Operating Expenses or Overheads. The salespeople will always tend to consider Gross Margin as their measure to care for and forget to cater to Overheads (as salespeople say, "Not our problem!"). This is contrary to the discussions held at the top management or Board levels, which always look at EBIT or EBITDA and not Gross Margin. Why should the focus be on different numbers at different levels of the organisation? Gross margins are not real profits of the business. EBIT and EBITDA are. So, every decision must be based on EBIT or EBITDA, including the choice to establish selling strategy and not on gross margins. It is imperative your business changes all Gross Margin- based decisions to EBIT-based.

EBITDA is Earnings before Interest, Taxes, Depreciation, and Amortization, and it is calculated as EBIT minus Depreciation and Amortisation (which are reported in the financials, both P & L & Balance Sheet). EBITDA is also referred to as Cash Profit and it reflects the effect of depreciation of capital equipment purchase on the EBIT. EBITDA will be almost the same as EBIT if there is no capital equipment investment or change in depreciation during the year.

Asset Turnover Ratio and Return on Total Assets

For all your capital investment decisions, please ensure that the assets being purchased deliver an Asset Turnover Ratio between 3 to 5 and Return on Total Assets of 12% to 17% once fully commissioned. Any returns below these ratios indicate underutilisation of the assets you purchased or over-capitalisation in the business (i.e., spending more than you require on the assets) and will contribute to cash flow issues and financial stress.

Debt to Equity Ratio and Leverage Ratio

Leverage Ratio indicates the extent of liabilities of current and long-term debt as compared to the equity of the owners. When you regularly monitor Leverage Ratio in combination with Debt-to-Equity Ratio, you can understand the risk profile of the owners; a Leverage Ratio continually higher than 2 shows uncontrolled debt and the lack of financial discipline. In other words, the business should be running on a balance of debt and equity as debt can help the business grow faster. A higher value than 2 indicates the business may not be very well managed and has been reckless in financial decision making and expenses (unless there is a valid explanation). On the other side, a value lower than 0.5 shows the risk profile of low debt acceptance; the business may not be using debt to grow its revenue. This needs to be analysed further as it may not be able to generate higher rate of returns than the interest it pays.

Value Add % and Creating Value Addition

A very important financial measure is the amount of value you are adding in your organisation to the costs that you incur to produce the goods and services you provide. The higher the Value Add %, the more profits you generate and the more premium you are able to command from your customers. Manufacturing can add higher than 60% to 80% premium, whereas trading or distributorship of other company's products generally will not add more than 30%. Please see detailed discussion in the section on Product Costing, Rule 16.

As a business providing a product or service, you bring in raw materials and other purchases to convert into products and service to provide to your customers at a price. Value Addition is defined as Selling Price of your Goods or Service MINUS Cost of Materials Input in the Goods or Service.

Let me explain it with an example of making potato chips. Potatoes cost, say, one dollar per kilogram, but when converted to packed potato chips, the product sells for thirty dollars per kilogram. If packaging costs two dollars, a value of twenty-seven dollars per kilogram has been added in the manufacturing plant to make the product sellable at a price acceptable to the customer.

The difference in the cost of buying potatoes and the selling price of the chips made from the potatoes, twenty-seven dollars, is the value addition done in your conversion processing. The value addition is directly linked to the processing carried out and reflects the level of premiumisation, manual labour content, technology used, automation, etc.

The importance of Value Addition is in the price your customers perceive and what they are prepared to pay for the goods and services. That price will decide whether you are going to play in the "premium" end of the market or the "price point" end of the market. More the Value Addition is seen the higher the customers will be prepared to pay (example of Louis Vuitton luxury brand leather handbags compared to other quality leather handbags) and the higher the net profitability of the goods and services. For businesses offering a service, providing free years of service in cars will add value and so increase the perception of better offering.

Another example is a farmer who sells their produce to the supermarkets and then starts producing cooked or processed and packaged products like soups under their own brands to the premium end of the market, increasing net profits. By converting the produce to soup, the farmer has created more value for the produce, has reduced wastage and opened up another channel for their products. The increased Value Addition has now increased their EBIT and also the brand awareness.

Once you become good at monitoring the financial health of your organisation, you will manage your cash flow very well. You do not need to depend only on your accountant to keep track of this on a periodic (at least monthly) basis. Just make sure they can provide you the financial ratios above and the trends of the ratios in your organisation, and you will be in control.

RULE 16

ENSURE PRODUCT/SERVICE COSTS ARE CORRECT TO PROVIDE REAL PROFITABILITY.

One of the most common weakness I have found has been people or companies not knowing the correct costs of the products and services they provide. 9 out of 10 of the SME businesses I have advised have not used correct costing methods to work out their costs and margins.

This rule maybe a bit complex for some but is very important to look at the profitability of your business/ section and to ensure you can increase your profits. To get the costing right, you may need the help of your accountant to prepare a basic, correct costing with the following components.

Itemised Components for Costing Products or Services

1) Cost of Goods Sold includes	Landed costs of all materials used for making the product
	Direct labour costs
	Cost of all other purchases
	Costs of the Subcontractors employed
	Manufacturing Overheads, also called Indirect and Variable Overheads

2) Operating Expenses or Overheads	Include all and every expense not part of COGS, like freight, energy, marketing, salaries, depreciation, R&D, rent, etc. Add the total of these and then calculate this as % of sales revenue figure. This % figure will be different for every financial year. TO ADD this into the Costings: Use this % figure to calculate the overheads addition to each costing. For the previous year and then ADD ONLY AT THE END. Otherwise you could add multiple times. This % will change annually so becomes a target to reduce.
Total product cost	Equals 1) plus 2)

All these components must be correctly understood and calculated to reach a correct costing of each product. As a very top-level thumb rule for total cost, we consider Materials comprising 50%, labour at 25%, and Overheads at 25%, but this would vary from industry to industry. Find your industry's data in benchmarking information from your industry association or refer to any reliable market data available.

Selling Revenue Price minus the Total Product cost will give us Net Profit margin, or EBIT, to be expressed as a %. Please remember EBIT % is also the opportunity cost of the capital employed in the business; if the EBIT is less than the bank interest you pay, then you are losing money.

Please consider this question "Do we always sell on net profit margins and not on gross profit?" Let me give you an example of a business I advise advised. When I asked how they were pricing their products, the owner indicated "we put a margin of 50% over the costs." When I calculated the EBIT% from the financials, they only had 3 % EBIT (or net profit before tax). Where did the 50% mark up disappear in actual profit & loss statement? Obviously the company was not taking into account all the costs components to get their costing and then have the correct sale price. Also, there were products which were providing high profits and there were some being sold on loss. That is to say, products sold on loss eat into the profits of company and is called "cannibalisation of profits." Why would you sell products or services at a loss? This affects your cash flow, inventory costs of loss-making products, wrong commissions, discount policies and strategies. It is very important to correct this problem immediately.

To check this out, work out all the costings clearly using correct fundamentals of a costing sheet. This is crucial for the survival of the business. This cost is the mainstay of the product pricing. Once it is done, then we work out the selling price strategies depending upon the market forces.

Calculate Net Profits of each SKU by using an Excel worksheet and see which SKUs are negative net profits. There are SKUs in your portfolio which_have selling prices, but which are not recovering all costs. Create the worksheet, and then sort the SKUs as per highest to lowest Net Profit basis. You can then look at the best and worst performers. Once you see negative or low profitability SKUs, then do any of the following: Increase the selling price to increase to a positive net margin, reduce costs for the SKU, eliminate the product, or be clear why you need to keep the prices the same and continue to sell below costs.

Don't be surprised if you find that a number of low or negative margin products are eating into the profits of your high-profit-margin SKUs This makes the overall business profits go down.

So if you are losing money or have low profits, check the details as per this rule out first. It may be the lowest hanging fruit to help solve your financial problems.

RULE 17

LEARN AND IMPLEMENT KEY PERFORMANCE MEASUREMENTS.

If you don't measure anything, then you are running blind. You can't change direction, and you will reach where you are headed: towards inconsistency and failure. This section will assist you in establishing Key Performance Indicators (KPIs) that will help you monitor the performance of yourself, the team, and the whole organisation.

It is crucial to understand what measurements help you on a daily basis. Let us look at the following diagram:

MEASURE → MONITOR → CONTROL → IMPROVE

ADVANTAGES OF MEASURING

If you measure the performance parameters then you can monitor the same, understand what is happening, and so control it and then improve upon it.

In all the organizations I worked in or have advised, I saw that performance numbers are not monitored in the same way across all levels in the company. What the board of directors measures and monitors is different from what the people down the line measure and regularly monitor.

Top management wants to measure numbers like EBIT, EBITDA, trends in sales revenue, performance against strategic goals, asset utilisation, debt to equity, leverage, etc., but staff are being measured on a daily basis on productivity (like labour efficiencies and maybe OEE), safety, gross margins, etc. Why do we have different KPIs? People will talk about different performance numbers at different levels and departments, making it almost impossible for common goal achievement or monitoring. When the company sets up a goal to achieve, why are all levels of the company using different targets?

What to Measure

What you should measure depends upon the type of business you are in. For every type of work, industry, and level of operations there are performance indicators that must be measured. There are many KPIs for each type of industry that one can select from to help implement the same. However, the various types of measures can be defined as:

a) **Lagging measures** (or post-outcome measurements) – Lagging KPIs indicate what has already occurred and measure indicators like profit, expenses, customer complaints received or customer returns, bad debts, etc. These are measures put in place to confirm or analyse what has already happened. These measurements are only taken post-delivery of the product or service and so donot predict change within without keeping track, which is mostly done by using leading indicators (see below).

b) **Leading indicators** (pre-outcome measurements) – Leading indicators tell you where your business is going. These measures are indicative of future performance that may affect, for example, customer satisfaction as we measure "Picking errors in stores" and "Delivery In Full On Time (DIFOT)," or the quality level consistency, which is indicated by a measure of variation like standard deviation.

c) **Absolute measures** – These indicators are number values of measurements like Total sales in $ (say $ 2,500,000 in sales), tonnes moved (say 100,000 Tonnes), or absolute of profit in dollars (say $ 100,000). These numbers seem to show a performance but have no context and can't explain if these are good or bad trends. They can only be compared *per se* to another number. While we can use these numbers to compare performance over year (last year vs. current year, for example), they are difficult to benchmark and do not convey meaningful decision-making data.

d) **Ratios** – A ratio measures a number relative to another number. Ratios make comparison easy. Using ratios is the best way to measure and monitor for the following reasons:

   i. A ratio allows comparison between two measures, making it easy to understand. Total labour cost this week, in dollars, compared to next week's total labour cost just shows bulk numbers; the comparison does not reflect whether the number of workers or their hours are same or different. Dividing the dollar amount by number of labours hours paid each time shows the cost per labour hour; now, productivity and comparison is possible.

ii. Ratios always will allow statistical analysis and so are predictable. You can plan and budget well with the growth.

iii. Ratios allow benchmarking comparisons to make the organisation aware of how they are faring as compared to competition.

iv. Ratios can be created for any two factors to convey comparisons ranging from simple to complex.

While there are hundreds of measures possible, many organisations will track these important KPIs in the table below.

Common KPIs

	Description	Details
Safety	Lost Time Injury Frequency Rate (LTIFR)	= Lost time injuries X 1,000,000 staff hours divided by hours worked
	Number of Near Misses	Every near-miss incident

Sales Growth	$ Revenue for the period	Measure every week, month, year
	% change over previous period	($ Revenue This Year – $ Revenue Last Year) / $ Revenue Last Year
Customer Service	Delivery in Full, On Time (DIFOT)	% of contracts or jobs delivered in the specified purchase order placed and defined time period
	Customer Complaints	Absolute numbers received per month
	Customer Complaints over units supplied	Number of complaints per million units supplied
Costings	Labour, %	Direct Labour Costs / $ Revenue
	Overheads, %	All Operating Expenses / $ Revenue
	Net Margin, %	EBIT and EBITDA
Waste	YIELD, %	(Weight kg of output produced) / (Weight kg of all input material components)
Manufacturing Performance of equipment lines (Productivity) See further explanation below	Overall Equipment Effectiveness (OEE) = Availability X Performance X Quality	**Availability** = Operating Time / Planned Production Time **Performance** = Ideal Cycle Time / (Operating Time / Total Pieces) **Quality** = Passed Pieces / Total Pieces

Quality	% Rework	Number of hours involved in remedying faulty work captured as % of total hours worked
Fleet Effectiveness	Modified Overall Vehicle Effectiveness	Vehicle Utilisation X Route Efficiency X Time Efficiency X Quality
Store Sales	Revenue per m^2	Revenue / Square Metre of retail space
Inventory	Stock Turns	Cost of Goods Sold (from P & L) / Stock on Hand
Financial	Value Addition done	(Revenue minus Cost of bought in materials and services) / Revenue
	EBIT, %	Earnings Before Interest & Tax / Revenue for the month
	EBITDA, %	Earnings Before Interest, Tax, Depreciation Amortisation / Revenue for the month
Social Media Effectiveness	ROI	Sales revenue increase online
Logistics & Warehouse	Delivery in Full on Time (DIFOT)- measured for each item supplied against the Purchase Order	Number of SKUs delivered on date / Number of SKUs ordered for the date
	Picking Errors, %	Indication of customer complaints, product returns, refunds, etc.

Standard Deviation	Variation from Average Performance	One of the most important measures in Control charts to show predictability (See also Rule 18 next)
Six Sigma	Normal Distribution Curve for the Data	Achieving operational excellence, zero errors and minimal variation. Essential for some industries like hospitals, airlines, etc. (See also Rule 18 next)

Important Notes to set KPIs:

There are general principles you can follow to make sure you are choosing KPIs effectively.

Avoid using gross margins measurements for sales decisions. Please see details in Rule 16 above.

Labour Efficiency & Machine Line Efficiency alone are not meaningful. Efficiency is a ratio measure of output against time. However, the output performance of any line is a combination of output quantity, the labour hours used, on the equipment they work with and the quality acceptable quantity that was passed to supply. So, the efficiency measure (which is just output against time) does not show the real picture. Any measure of productivity must relate to the product or service outcome that can be provided to the customer, as the outcome is what the customer pays for. So, calculating efficiency without considering the quality of the outcome is an incomplete measure. A worker producing rejects is worse than one not producing at all as rejects don't get paid for by the customer, there are reworking costs to bring them to acceptable quality, and they require replacement materials. The only measure that has any meaningful performance measurement is OEE (see note below). That is the best measure for a manufacturing or processing environment.

Measure Overall Equipment Effectiveness (OEE):

OEE measures the effectiveness of the equipment in adding value. The overall performance of a single piece of equipment or even an entire factory, will always be governed by the cumulative impact of the three OEE factors: Availability, Performance and Quality. Measuring OEE is considered as implementing best practice and will improve the whole manufacturing processes and ROI on investments done on equipment assets.

OEE = Availability (A) X Performance (P) X Quality (Q),

Where

Availability (A)=Actual Running Time of the equipment operation / Total operating time planned

Performance (P) = Actual quantity output in a day / Expected standard quantity in a day

Quality (Q) =   Quantity accepted by quality inspection / Actual quantity output in a day

For example, to calculate OEE for the day, let us take the following given data:

1) Total operating time planned in a day: 8 hours (single shift)

2) Actual Running Time: 7 hours (and 1 hour lost in downtime of the equipment)
3) Actual quantity output in the hours worked: 80 pieces
4) Expected standard quantity in same time: 100 pieces
5) Quantity passed by quality dept.: 75 pieces (i.e. 5 pieces are rejected)

Calculating:

Availability (A) = 7 / 8 = 87.5% (0.875)

Performance (P) = 80 / 100 = 80% (0.8)

Quality (Q) = 75 / 80 = 93.75% (0.9375)

So OEE: A X P X Q = 0.875 X 0.8 X 0.9375 = 0.656 = 65.6%

So, we are only achieving 65.6% effectiveness of our line on the particular day.

Generally, it is accepted that world class best performing companies get a value of 85% OEE so benchmarking can be done. One % improvement in OEE directly hits the bottom line so any improvement increases profitability.

A large number of measures adds complexity and division. The more measures you have, the more division there is between departments. When departments set up their own KPIs, the targets may or may not be compatible and even in conflict with others being used in the organisation, and so measurement becomes counterproductive. The best measure for responsibility and accountability, first, is an overall EBITDA% or EBIT% target for the business. Then work backwards to set up localised section targets, all of which will then contribute to the EBITDA/EBIT. If the targets of sections or departments clash and do not lead to one EBITDA/EBIT target, then the business is setting up silos and adding pressures. So, keep one encompassing KPI for the business and work back from there to introduce sectional targets, think RAAT, so that everyone works towards one goal.

Use statistics carefully. Statistics is a language that can be twisted to suit any interpretation if selectively presented. So, keep the KISS principle in mind when presenting the data: Keep It Simple and Straight. Always present the data visually so correct representation is done without creating any distortion of facts. However, we should look at Statistical Process Control Charts (SPC charts) to measure real time live on data to measure variations as they happen. Please see the next section, Rule 18, on data measurements.

Consult Further Reading for books and resources on these concepts, indicated in the book resources list at 11,12,13,14, 27, 28, 29.

RULE 18

IMPROVE MANUFACTURING/ OPERATIONS PROCESSES BY IMPLEMENTING VISUAL CONTROLS.

In manufacturing, especially, our processes in equipment, new or old, keep chugging away. But do we really know that our processes are in control? All processes vary on a natural basis indicated by Process Variation. Most often we take action when we think the process is not in control, when in fact these variations are part of the statistical control limits of the process. You can understand the extent of variation and use standard deviation calculations to predict how the process will be performing, for example, in terms of average piece weight.

How should you record and use that process variation measurements to enable you to get control over the process? More often we would rather record the measurement in a table as a number rather than plot it on a graph as seen below. Here, let us see the measurements below as in table format.

Process Measurements Table

Time	Relative Humidity, %	Weight of the 10 product samples	Average Weight of the samples
7.30	47	141	14.1
8.30	51	122	12.2
9.30	57	130	13
10.30	53	140	14
11.30	47	131	13.1
12.30	41	160	16
13.30	46	153	15.3
14.30	54	123	12.3
15.30	58	129	12.9
16.30	61	139	13.9

The table above hardly offers insight into the behaviour of the process numbers. Are the number going up or down, or are they trending, and in which direction? Is there a pattern? Are they within specs or outside specs? The absolute numbers need to be worked upon to get meaningful information for the quality levels in inspection and also the customer giveaway. (Customer giveaway is the excess quantity that you give away to the customers in packs you supply, As in example above, the 125gm packs shows an average pack weight of 136.8gms across ten samples which means 11.8gms is going extra to the customers on an average in every pack approx. 9.44% extra for free. Multiply that over a ton of supply and the quantity comes to between 94.4 kg extra stock per tonne which can be a huge cost if not kept in control. In the example above, some are getting less too and some are getting far more, which can be an legal issue under the pack weights trades regulations.

You can't deduce any thing easily out of the data table, but if you plot the data in graphical presentation as below then you can easily understand the trends and variation. There are several types of plots and diagrams that we can transform this data into. One example is the histogram. By simply plotting the recordings as shown below (you can use graph paper or Microsoft Excel), a picture emerges and you see a trend. The visual plot now shows much better variation for control and analysis. Here, we have plotted the numbers from the table into a histogram bar chart.

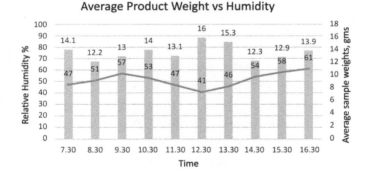

HISTOGRAM BAR CHART

Similarly, the calculations of the weights in the table's last column do not indicate anything wrong with the process. Plot it as control chart, however, and you see a different picture, as shown below in the control chart.

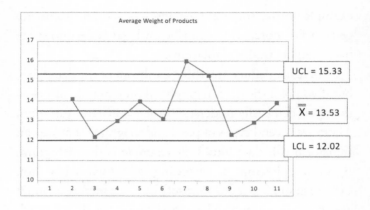

CONTROL CHART

The graph above shows the trend being followed by the data and whether it is meeting the specifications or not. You can also see the extent of variation, if there are very high fluctuations or slight ones. Using this information, you can establish the control limits and specification limits to ensure products are always within them. You can even predict what the next reading will be by using the SPC computations and calculating standard deviation.

Statistical Process Control (SPC) charts (as first devised by Shewhart) provide answers to understand the difference between Stable Process Variations (which need no action at all) and Out of Control Process Variations (which will need to have worker's intervention action to stabilize the process).

Control charts are based on certain sampling methods and most often are very easy to establish. Control charts are the way to understand whether the process is in control or not. There are many types of control charts, and the table below gives the most common ones.

Types of Control Charts

Main types of variation measurements	Statistical Process Control chart	Brief description
Variables Control Charts	Average Chart (also called the Xbar chart)	When samples data are in quantitative measurements numbers like weight, temperature, metres, ratios etc.
	Range Chart	The difference between highest and lowest measure data at any time period.
Attributes Control Charts	p-Chart	When samples data is in qualitative characteristics like number of dents or marks on surface, go or no-go, etc.
	np-Chart	
	c-Chart	
	u-Chart	

To implement SPC, you need to consult any management statistical book or various websites. The best books on this are by CRC Press (https://www.routledge.com/), also known as A Productivity Press part of Taylor & Francis Group.

In conclusion, tabulated data and Control Charts are as comparable as a still photograph and a video. Single measurements are like still photographs taken over time—good but not good enough as it leaves gaps in time. The Control Chart is the video which gives life to the moment;

you can see what was happening all the while and you can even predict the records.

Today there is a massive usage of digital data collection and analysis and now AI is playing a big part. Creating a DASHBOARD of key areas is crucial for any performance monitoring and that could be put on display on a screen in any organization on real time basis.

Please see the book resources list in Further Reading, specifically 11, 12, 13, 14, 16.

RULE 19

IDENTIFY WASTES AND TAKE ACTION TO REDUCE THEM.

Waste is misunderstood. In almost all organisations that I have worked in I found that people understood waste as the product wastage that is not sellable and dumped at the end of the day.

Whenever I ask the question "What is the waste level built into your product costings?" the answer usually is "We don't have much waste" or "We think it is between 1% to 5%" or "We don't know." In organisations with enterprise resource planning (ERP) systems, the costing sheet may not contain any wastage factor. It is such a common problem, however, that companies implement Lean manufacturing strategy and action plans to try to understand waste and improve yields i.e. to calculate ratio of weight of the output to inputs, which is also another way to understand waste. In other words, a 5% waste would mean a yield of 95%.

Besides product waste, there are many other types of waste that people don't even consider. Eight types of waste have been defined, and all come with a cost. The more waste you have of each type, the more costs are borne by the business and the less profit there is. You can remember the eight types of waste by using DOWNTIME, as derived from Toyota Production System (TPS) as an acronym, as below:

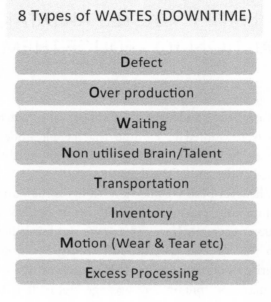

8 Types of WASTES (DOWNTIME)

Defect

Over production

Waiting

Non utilised Brain/Talent

Transportation

Inventory

Motion (Wear & Tear etc)

Excess Processing

EIGHT TYPES OF WASTES

Defects: These are imperfections or out-of-specifications in the products or services produced. These may be acceptable defects, allowed by the standards, or unacceptable defects, which lead to rejects or returns.

Overproduction: Overproduction occurs when a line produces products when it is made to run even when not required just to utilise labour available or utilise the material, even when next stage does not require the output product.

Waiting: Waiting occurs when people wait for materials or a machine, or a machine waits for labour – in both circumstances, there is idle time. Both labour and machines are waiting to be used.

Non-utilised brains or talent: This is the most ignored waste type, as a result of management not engaging with the workforce or teams not taking advantage of all the members to solve a problem. Multiple brains are more useful than a single person's brain. Teams always will be more effective, as seen in all models of employee engagement.

Transportation: In a process, transportation waste occurs when there is excessive movement of people, materials, products, etc., causing unnecessary movement, double-handling, time delays, waiting delays, and workforce fatigue. Reduction of such movement improves on the cycle time and improves working conditions within the area.

Inventory: Higher inventory hides many underlying problems in planning and procurement, in stock keeping inaccuracies, improving DIFOT, forecasting problems, etc. The biggest cost to management comes from liabilities, due to higher payables to the suppliers as well as lifecycle costs and waste. Higher inventory is an asset but blocks cash, so keeping inventory to the minimum allows a business to reduce its cash-to-cash cycle as well as reduce issues with multiple handling of the inventory stock. Just-in-Time processes and receiving inventory right when it is needed reduces many issues of higher inventory.

Motion (Wear and Tear, etc): All equipment undergoes wear and tear during use. These issues are compounded by improper maintenance, lack of preventive care, etc. Further, unnecessary and non-essential movement, excessive speed, multiple handling and movements all lead to higher time loss, non-essential distance travel, and more wear and tear.

Excess Processing: Using more processing time than required (e.g., overnight running when is not required till morning) or creating more steps in a process than necessary, or even allowing higher-specification tolerance levels than required by the customer, leads to higher costs and wastage of energy, more wear, etc.

The Lean manufacturing methodology is actually the best system to understand waste in your organisation and to implement the systems that change the culture with regards to waste reduction. It is the most effective way of attacking waste in any organisation, be it manufacturing, agriculture, banks, public sector or government, healthcare, etc. There are thousands of examples of companies changing their productivity and culture spread from global icons like Toyota, General Electric as well as in thousands of SMEs all over the world. Proper execution & implementation is the key in SMEs as three factors of execution (see book 2 in further reading) always work – strategy, right people and proper operations.

Waste reduction should become a continuous improvement activity all across the company. Analysis of each of the eight wastes in your organisation is essential to start reducing them. As each of the above eight wastes contribute to costs, you really want to attack waste seriously to get the benefits of reduced costs, improved yields, improved inventory levels, increased productivity, higher outputs with better utilisation of equipment and lines.

It is important to understand that LEAN methodology is very useful for any function of any organization - be it sales, service, finance (Banks use it a lot to reduce costs and improve service response time) etc.

Consult Further Reading for books and resources on these concepts, indicated in the book resources list at 2, 13, 14, 15, 20, 21.

RULE 20

GROW YOURSELF AS A LEADER.

You cannot grow in business if you do not grow as a leader capable of leading intelligent, professional people and teams. I have seen that single-owner companies with rigid micromanagement do not grow beyond a certain level in revenue and size when the owner cannot let go and cannot delegate authority. The resulting limitation of time and resources prevents the business from becoming a larger company.

As a leader, you need to grow as a person, as a leader, and as a follower. Do not think small; always think in terms of the bigger picture. Do you understand how your role affects the performance of the section, unit, plant, company, and the organisation, or do you take responsibility only for your own tasks? Do you look at the people above you to understand their personality, their values and beliefs, and the culture they create? Do you honestly see yourself and your self-beliefs as good enough for leading people in your current role? Your personal development and growth are far more important than just of the people around you. If you lack the knowledge, skills set or technology required to do your job and respond to what is happening around you, then you have a problem.

My personal rules that have helped me a lot are as below.

1) **Always think big.** Be a big-picture person and avoid getting bogged down in small thinking. I recommend the book *Magic of Thinking Big* by David J. Schwartz; everyone must read it to understand that one must strive towards excellence and not just depend upon circumstances and luck to let things happen as they do. Reliance Industries, India is an example of a company that likes to think in global terms. When they were setting up their first petroleum oil refinery in Jamnagar, India, they decided to make it the world's largest. Jamnagar refinery was set up in record time in 1999. There are many examples and I will enumerate a few that I have advised – a small fresh pasta company in Victoria by thinking big, it has grown from a $3 million company to a $15 million company in five years. A metal recycling company in Victoria has put a strategy to grow global in circular economy and become a $ 1 billion conglomerate in next 10 years.

2) **Don't take any important decisions in life in moments of weakness.** All important decisions need to be taken with thoughts behind them and never when you are feeling down or under stress. If you have any of the three types of stresses—financial, time, or mental—you don't want to be taking on anything new or making changes in your life to increase your stress.

3) **Be Disciplined. Failure is given if this is not followed.** Build your mental strength to become disciplined and follow your own rules. Disciplines bring in consistency of behaviour and people will understand they can predict and trust your behaviour once they see this from you. If you act without being disciplined person, you are setting yourself for failures.

4) **Take no shortcuts ever.** If you have habit of taking shortcuts in actions or on your path, you are setting up for failure. If you do everything right and follow principles, you cannot fail, even though you may have hiccups.

5) **Look after the business when a crisis strikes.** Survival is the basic instinct but look beyond yourself. Look after people, your brand, control discretionary spending, conserve cash, and look for government support. In any crisis, you need to move in fast to act to protect people, assets and brand.

6) **Follow the adage "We will cross that bridge when we come to it."** Priotise worrying about issues based on urgency and not on issues that are too far away in time to occur.

7) **Pat yourself at the back once in a while.** Reward yourself when you achieve milestones and have proud moments. Take time out to celebrate with your staff when celebrations are due.

8) **Take action to overcome the fear.** "Action kills fear" is espoused by Skip Ross, author of "Say Yes to your Potential – Skip Ross Magic Formula for

Dynamic *Living*. If you have any fear of something happening, then take action to overcome the fear. You cannot solve every fear, but you will always come out well if you *act* to overcome the fear. I can give many examples but one that stands out is from my time in charge of a food manufacturing company, when an employee came to me and said sheepishly that she tasted a product from the line and discovered a piece of plastic in it. She was sorry that she had broken the no-tasting rule but could not keep this information to herself. Her fear was that, while she would be spoken to harshly, the damage to the company would be greater punishment to her as by chance she found the contamination occurring. She overcame her fear and acted to stop the production happening on the line. The product was put on quarantine and an investigation was carried out to identify the source of plastic. It was a broken piece from a small bracket in the equipment. The investigation showed the damage was not extensive as repairs had just been carried out two hours earlier and not a lot of stock needed to be rejected due to the contamination. Her action helped the company. Of course, the employee was advised to not break the no-tasting rule again, but she was also appreciated publicly for taking the actions she did.

Ask Yourself:

☐ What kind of focus do you have in your respective role? Is it just around your own narrow network, closed sphere of influence or you think global?

☐ Do you look up to the senior leadership in your organisation to compare your skill set to theirs? Do you like what you see?

☐ Is the culture you propagate better for the people and organisation? Do you follow your own rules?

For further study, see the book resources list in Further Reading at 1, 4, 6, 7, 8, 9, 10, 30, 33, 34.

RULE 21

MAKE NETWORKING THE KEY FOR MARKETING AND BUILDING RELATIONSHIPS.

Networking is the art of developing relationships with people on a large scale to help build your circle of influence, friendships, acquaintances, business colleagues, mentors, common interest groups, etc.

Networking is crucial for personal and professional growth. Many people fear networking. I was, too, and I suffered in my career for it. A friend who was at a senior level in banking told me that he always kept one day a week, preferably Friday evening, free for networking. He would arrange coffee with the people who mattered in his organisation or who worked in other organisations in the same field, or attended events arranged by professional bodies to associate with colleagues. He enabled his career with these contacts and continued to rise. I could not take his advice for some specific reasons and so I was late by almost 5 years getting into my advisory roles. I have no regrets, but I could have been happier earlier with a longer consultancy role in life.

Here are the rules for building a strong network:

1) **Be genuinely interested in helping others.** If you look at what is good for you first, you will never form a good, genuine network. Always think how you can help the people or companies you want to network.

2) **Be generous.** If you find anything of interest to someone you know— market news or an item concerning their business or skill set or an article on issues that affect their growth, anything related to them or their business—send them the details or the link.

3) **Send greetings.** If you have developed a personal relationship, then wish them good tidings on their birthday. If it is not yet a good relationship, please decide if you should send them a message or not; however, if there is a tragedy in their family, then you must convey commiseration.

4) **Be an active networker.** Because you must look for ways to help people, you are networking every moment of your life, and to do that, you keep a look out all the time.

5) **Pay attention to all the networking channels.** Networking happens all the time. You should be using social media but also the proven most practical ways. Join the professional industry association your business is in. Do a course with a professional body and stay in touch with the alumni of any college or the professional course you did. Attend meetings of the association,

local commerce chamber or any organisation conducting programmes. Start playing golf or a sporting activity.

6) **Set aside time for networking.** Try to keep an evening or afternoon free every week or fortnight to build your network. Set up meeting times to catch up with people to help mutually both your businesses, growth, and circle. A win-win for both. Attend trade shows, exhibitions and seminars to expand your network.

7) **Use social media networking tools.** Today you can use so many methods to communicate: Whatsup, Facebook, LinkedIn, emails, messages, broadcasts, podcasts etc etc. Use them all to stay in touch with your network but do not pester them or bombard them with unnecessary messages. Do unto them what you would like to be done to you. Leave positive remarks for people on Facebook, Twitter, LinkedIn, etc. This activity is more crucial than writing your own posts. Form or join LinkedIn groups for business conversations.

8) **Remember: Networking is for working on your business and personal growth.**

RULE 22

FOLLOW THE 6 PS TO
BE EXIT READY.

When in business, the golden rule should be Always Be Exit Ready. What is meant by *exit ready*? And why? Exit ready is a state in which the company can be taken over by external investors, or in other words, sold, to enable owners achieve best value for the business that has been built. In normal, daily operations, the question always arises as to what the value of the business is. Different valuation methods can be used, but the best value is attained when the organisation can run effectively without the owners or the top management but also has good cashflow, net assets, above average EBIT/EBITDA, growth potential, effective second- and third-tier leadership, strategic activities and so on. There are thousands of SMEs in a situation that I remember seeing with an elderly couple who were eagerly depending upon their children to take over the business by buying them out. Unfortunately, none of children were keen to follow them into business. The owners had left it too late to become exit ready and get a good valuation. They struggled to find a buyer for the business, and the gentleman passed away, leaving his wife to run it. Needless to say, the business collapsed, and no value was received. If only they had listened to this advice and prepared themselves and their business to be exit ready!

The following 6 Ps will assist you in reaching exit-ready status.

Plan

From the day you decide you want to exit, it will take you 2-3 years, normally. So, you need to plan for it. The planning process starts with a detailed financial analysis of the organisation (or department as a standalone business), including the P&L and the balance sheet, all numbers that reflect it as an independent business. Then, benchmark your organisation to others in your industry to show you the gap between your organisation and the industry average. You should be able to get information on similar businesses from IBIS reports or benchmarking data providers.

Prepare

Now we start preparing the organisation to fill in the gaps we identified in benchmarking or general industry comparison. Establish a strategic business plan with goals for the business at the exit time. What are the goals for sales revenue, EBIT/EBITDA, net profit before tax, current/quick ratio, operating expense (overheads) ratio, etc.? Set goals to become the best performing business in your industry—or world-class if that data comparison is possible. Exit ready must include how you would exit a partnership / shareholder in a business in order to avoid litigation.

People

The most important aspect of exit readiness is understanding the skill level of business you have built. Can the business operate without you being present there to direct it? If everyone is depending upon one individual to take all decisions, then you don't have an organisation that is worth much. So, creating a workforce with enough defined, documented and implemented RAAT (see Rule 6- Responsibility-Accountability – Authority-Trust) is crucial. Creating second- and third-tier leadership who can run the organisation effectively will be of utmost responsibility of the top management. What are the staffing levels, and who will be doing what? Establishing that along with a training policy and skill matrix (see Rule 9), with performance KPIs and monitoring systems (Rule 17) will help you create a self-managed team environment that can run the organisation when the leadership exits.

Protect

We need to protect the assets for long-term operation of the business. The assets are defined as:

- **physical assets** like equipment, infrastructure, stocks. They need to be in a clearly defined asset register with clear ownership state and with details of financial liability on them. Your tax return's P&L and Balance Sheet will, and should, contain full details. Check your balance sheet and depreciation schedules. If the asset is not listed you won't get the ownership of them at exit stage.

- **intellectual property**, like trademarks and copyrights must be protected by registration, if applicable. Any trade secrets should be clearly kept in safe custody with defined accountability and authority.
- **other people's assets**, Need documentation for stocks not paid for, dies and tools on the premises which belong to customers or others, any equipment loaned to others or on loan from others, any money lying as an accrual with you (advance payments, etc.) are all some types of assets that can be in doubtful ownership situations.
- **technology assets**. Cybersecurity is crucial to protect your IT systems with adequate security and password policy and data transfer blockages. Hire experts to help. Link with cloud services only from global companies like Google, Amazon, Microsoft etc. Do not use a small local IT server etc. You are responsible for any hacking anywhere else that may occur due to your IT systems.

Protection of assets also comes from adequate insurance and coverage with reputable insurance company and of the replacement value of the assets. This is one activity where any shortchanging will not help as claims may not provide value if the policy is not adequate. Review the policy every year for the content and value along with the premium.

Project for Future

No business is of value if there is no planning for growth. Starting with an aspirational model, it will be good to lay out what you want the business to look like in the next four to five years. The detailed business plan will be the next step. You can prepare it using the Business Canvas model and then prepare a projected P&L. Aim for a minimum of 25% growth from new products, EBIT of 10%, EBITDA of 10% to15%, and the NPAT higher than the bank interest rate for short-term loans.

Profit

No business is exit ready if there is no profit. Measurements in EBIT, EBITDA, and NPAT will need to be always positive and straightforward, not subjects of creative accounting. Ensure that all profits have the equity portion presented in the balance sheet as net assets. This shows you are investing back into the business. Take a salary and dividends from the business but retain enough to keep growing the net assets. The business must have a clean projection of profits to enable a good valuation and sale.

There are some very good resources available from the Exit Planning Institute (https://exit-planning-institute. org/resources/bookstore) to help you become exit ready and ensure you come out on top when you decide to exit.

UNDERSTAND THE SUPPLY CHAIN AND ITS COSTS.

Do you fully understand what is meant by the complete supply chain that you are operating within? Where does it start? Where does it end? What is the total cycle time of your supply chain?

Let us start with definition first. A supply chain, according to APICS Operations Management Body of Knowledge Framework (http://www.apics.org/docs/default-source/industry-content/apics-ombok-framework.pdf), is defined as "the whole supply line of any product or service from start is described as a supply chain." In other words, it is the start of a product being processed to reaching the consumer as the finish line. For example, a vegetables supply chain will start from a farmer growing the produce, then to transport it to a distributor warehouse, which then further get transported to retail super market, where it will be sold to a consumer who will take it home to consume. This farm to consumer home journey is a supply chain.

The diagram below shows the full supply chain for a fresh vegetable-based soup product consumed by a customer, basically a farm-to-table chain.

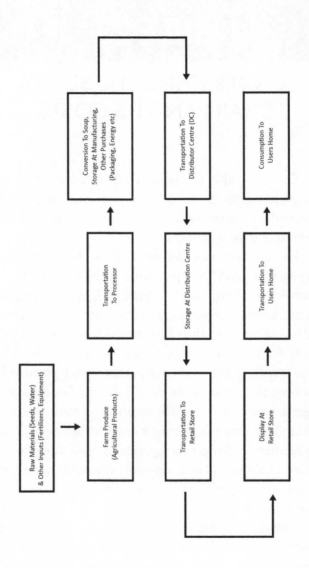

SUPPLY CHAIN DIAGRAM

The diagram besides indicates the full value stream of seeds (raw materials, water, fertilisers, etc.), which produce the vegetables, the transportation of produce to manufacturing, its conversion to a soup product, the transportation of soup to the Distribution Centre (DC), storage at DC, then transportation to Retail Store (RS), display at RS, the purchase by the consumer, transportation to the consumer's home, and then the product is finally consumed. So, you can see that the complete supply chain constitutes various components:

- **Costs**, which are incurred at many stages and which are paid for by the consumer when they buy the product.
- **Waste and/or loss**, occurring throughout the stages of the supply chain, which will be paid for by the company who ultimately may or may not charge the customers.
- **Infrastructure**, as in warehouses/ distribution centres to maintain an effective supply chain.
- **Logistics**, which includes transport systems in road, rail, water, oceans, or air, stretching from human-pulled delivery rickshaws to ships.
- **Freight**, as a major component of the external service providers influencing the price and selling cycle inventory.
- **Environment conditions**, which become crucial in decision-making to remain competitive, and which are based upon the products being moved in the supply chain. Like bulk movement for mines or agriculture products like grains and

pulses, cold chains for frozen or chilled products, or temperature-based and bio secure chains for pharmaceuticals etc.

- **Reverse logistics** for return of products, say, due to rejects and recalls, which will be paid for by the business supplying the product.
- **Technology**, which touches the products at each stage – in storage, transportation, manufacturing, in display in various forms and processes (scanning, data entry, shelf-life control, etc.), all of which require capital equipment and software licensing investments. Use of Enterprise Resource Planning (ERP) softwares to help manage the whole supply chain is essential.
- **Human** (and robotic) touches at multiple points.
- **The total cycle time**, which determines the total financials required, and which needs to be minimised to manage the cash flow.
- **Management of the supply chain effectively** contributes to the selling costs, inventory control, stock obsolescence, delivery costs, delivery times, picking errors, returns & recalls, freight costs etc. So it is very important to manage it well. See Rule 24 below too.

For you to be competitive, you will need to minimise the costs and wastes.

We can have the various supply chains constituted or split in various forms as below:

- Supplier's Supplier to Customer's Customer (final User)

- Cash Out to Cash In Cycle (e.g., purchasers invoice payments to debtor's payment receipt)
- Farm linked, whereby raw inputs supply into the farm to produce delivery to processor, e.g., "Farm to Plate")
- Manufacturing linked, whereby raw materials move into manufacturing (processing and packaging equipment) for conversion to Finished Goods (FG), then FG by transport Logistics to Distribution Warehouse to Retailer,
- Retail linked, product into Distribution Warehouse Centre to Retail Store shelf.

Supply chain management is very crucial and a vast subject and much beyond the scope of this book. There is not a single university that teaches business that does not teach this subject. There are so many members associations and organisations covering the supply chain that there is no paucity of knowledge resources. Seek out the best member organisation for your business to learn and master your supply chain and its costs. I feel APICS provides the best resources with its courses.

Ask Yourself:
- ☐ Which part of the supply chain do you contribute to in your field of activity/ role?
- ☐ Do you understand the various components and costs of that supply chain and how they determine the actual user cost or price point?
- ☐ What technology do you have to manage and monitor the supply chain as compared to your competition?

MAKE INVENTORY MANAGEMENT THE KEY.

One of the most important roles of the middle manager in supply chain management is inventory of goods. The company can be making profit or loss depending upon how the inventory is handled. Phrases like stockturns, ABC classification, scheduling deliveries, and consignment stocks start to hold importance due to their role in your product or service costs. Above all, we need to understand cash flow and how to manage it.

APICS Operations Management Body of Knowledge Framework (found at http://www.apics.org/docs/default-source/industry-content/apics-ombok-framework.pdf) says at item 5.2:

> "Inventory is listed as an asset on a firm's balance sheet and consists of the stocks or items needed to maintain production, support activities such as maintenance and repairs, and provide customer service. Inventory typically is categorised based on its flow through the production cycle as raw materials, work in process, and finished goods."

The importance of inventory is described below:

- Inventory is the most important asset maintained in any company involved in the supply chain.
- Money is needed to purchase, produce, store, and use inventory. If you keep high levels of inventories, you have used up more money cash to buy and keep in storage. So, high inventory lying in storage directly contributes to cash flow problems.
- Inventory must be correctly costed at each stage to have a correct valuation on the asset side of balance sheet.
- Inventory is crucial to all the financials statements of the business, Profit and Loss, Balance Sheet, and Cash Flow.
- Inventory needs to be planned and controlled very methodically in any business, be it in manufacturing, retail, or service. Optimisation of inventory by efficient procurement policies and systems with effective ordering quantities in regular cycle periods is essential.
- Different categorisations of inventory will create different valuations, and so optimisation and agility come from how much of the inventory is in raw materials (RM), work in process (WIP) or finished goods (FG). For example, FG is the highest costed item of the three, and keeping a high inventory of FG to manage customer service will block a lot of money till it is sold and money is received from the customer.

So, planning and control of inventory is the most important action of any leadership. APICS or any supply chain specialist will detail out the processes and tools involved to ensure you optimise the purchase costs, carrying costs, and overall inventory values. How much inventory do you need to keep and manage?

Type of Inventory Model

First of all, you need to understand what types of inventory models are applicable to your industry:

- Made to Order means making products only when customer order is received.
- Made to Stock requires you to establish production or stocking on a regular basis, based on the customer's delivery schedules and demand cycles and based on orders or contracts.
- Retail works on principles of "Buy–Stock–Sell," "What Gets Displayed Gets Sold" and "Fashion/ Fad/Trends," and inventory needs to be managed very effectively to keep the stock cycle short, so obsolescence and taste trends don't create waste and high discounts. There are some good books on the subject if you want to know more.
- Shelf Life becomes very crucial for the inventory model as food items or medical products are controlled purely by this.

I would like to give an example to show the importance of inventory management. I see a lot of companies not following their own policies properly. A company I advised, used a lot packaging from overseas in containers. Insufficient control of stock turns (a ratio indicating number of times the inventory turns over in a year - 1 means one year long stock and 12 means a month's inventory) was in place, and so excessive stocks of products were ordered covering for almost one year's requirement. A lot of money was stuck in inventories leading to huge cashflow problems.

Inventory management can be huge game changer for any company so we must use science. Starting with purchasing, the Ordering Inventory (for items that are normally required constantly) could be based on Economic Order Quantity (EOQ) generally for optimised lot purchase sizes. The formula is

$$EOQ = \frac{dTC}{dQ} = \sqrt{\frac{2SD}{H}}$$

EOQ FORMULA

where D = Annual Demand, S = Cost per order (\$), H = Holding cost (\$). H is calculated from IH X C where IH = Inventory Holding cost % and C = cost per unit in \$ of item being ordered.

Using EOQ is not feasible for every type of inventory as it assumes conditions like demand is constant through out etc, but it could be a starting place for optimising or minimising the inventory levels and numbers of orders to be placed in a year to manage ordering cycles effectively.

Please see any number of publications on this subject, especially by APICS.

Concept of ABC Categorisation

Inventory management is best done by categorising all inventory items under ABC classifications. To use this method, we need to identify each item as A, B or C. The table shows the most basic form with the last column showing "Example Order Frequency" i.e. the ordering cycles based on the categories.

ABC Categories

Category	Description	Example Order Frequency
A	Fast moving RM item or FG, most commonly required or ordered	Daily/Weekly/ Monthly
B	RM or FG required or ordered less frequently	Monthly/Every 3 Months
C	RM or FG required or ordered very infrequently	Monthly/Every 3 Months/Every 6 Months

How you decide to categorise inventory as A, B, or C will depend also on other factors like:

- Cost of the item: if items are of high costs, higher frequency ordering with smaller quantities will help keep costs lower.

- Lead time – Higher lead times items will need lower frequency of orders and will lead to higher inventory.
- Capacity constraints – The inability to manufacture or process stocks efficiently will determine the category. i.e. once a month or every three months or six months will determine the category and may require higher inventory levels.

Inventory Costing is another subject and will need accounts and supply chain experts to help you to minimise it.

RULE 25

MAKE QUALITY AS A JOURNEY OF CONSISTENCY:

You reap what you sow.

Quality of your products and services is one of the most important aspect of your commercial business life. It is best described by the GIGO principle- Garbage in garbage out. The quality of the output that you will produce will help provide you the customers you want to supply to, the market you want to enter and the reputation you want to build. If you want to play in premium price range you will need to ensure you use higher quality inputs so the price is no more the issue. In your every day role you will be faced with decisions on this subject continuously. Mastering this subject knowledge will keep you ahead of competition. If you let the quality down then you are on road to disaster.

Every business that I work with tells that they always supply quality product. No one ever says they make a bad quality product or service. The definition of *quality* is "fitment to purpose," which means the quality is what one considers as the acceptable level of risk in your organisation. The quality level for a hospital is different from what a stone crusher will find acceptable as the risk level in a hospital is much higher with lives at stake. If you deal in any quality product with high consistency, your customers will start to like what you offer as they can depend upon the quality. The moment they see quality but high variations, they will not be able to trust the supply coming in and so won't offer you the right price or a long-term contract. So good premium quality consistently maintained will be worth the effort.

Who is responsible for quality? Everyone. All people in the organisation must perform with defined quality levels so that extra quality inspectors are not needed to look over the shoulders and check VAP staff's line of work. This does not mean quality inspection work is never needed, it all depends upon the tolerance levels required, control of the error levels and above all the failure risks of high impact and high likelihood. Each person is responsible for their own quality performance. In processing, if the person in next stage of the processing checks the quality level and accepts it or sends the product back, then this stops any bad product going forward.

Your quality unique selling proposition (USP) is defined by:

- The minimum quality standard that you define and follow
- The average levels of the acceptable specifications and measures in each input material you use
- The variation allowed in the specifications in RM, WIP and FG, and
- The final quality specifications range that you promise to your customer.

But quality is a journey that one accepts to undertake to decrease the risk. The quality journey strongly recommended is described best here:

1) **Improve base quality:** The base quality one usually sees in an organisation starts from the raw materials or ingredients you use. The *garbage-in-garbage-out* principle means bad quality inputs can't produce good quality products or services. If you have large variations due to process inefficiencies, then you are forced to have loose or wider specifications causing inconsistencies in products produced.

2) **Attain consistency:** Standardise all processes and workers performing them on the floor by Standard Operating Procedures (SOPs) and Work Instructions (WI). Certify against the appropriate recognised global standards like ISO9000, Occupational Health & Safety (ISO45001), Environmental Standard (ISO 14001), Food Safety (ISO 22000), etc.

3) **Improve variation control:** Use design and measurement tolerance levels of third or fourth decimals (0.0000) to improve quality offering. Implement Statistical Control Charts (see Rule 18) to reduce process variation by real time-basis plotting of charts on the line of Average, Range, etc. Understand the power of Standard Deviations and Normal Distribution Curve. (For details and complete range of charts please see https://asq.org/ quality-resources/statistical-process-control.)

At the start, I recommend you implement manual, paper-driven control charts. There is software available to help, and you can run a Google search for the most appropriate software for your industry. The best level of variation control is by using Six Sigma techniques. Six Sigma stands for 6 standard deviations (as represented in writing by the Greek letter sigma, 'σ') from the mean or average. Each level from 1 sigma to 6 sigma, defines levels of errors or defects, which are reflected by the deviation of the measured data from the mean or average. It represents the percentage of defects allowed within the process. Every process can be broken down into the error levels accepted. For example, in a machine producing any part, if you are at 1 sigma level, you would be creating, approximately 69%, only good products and balance 31% are with defects every day. As you go up in the Six Sigma levels, you decrease the number of defects, and so rejects decrease, too, as do the costs, thus increasing your profits. Represented below in a normal distribution curve (also called bell curve due to its shape) are the error levels at various standard deviations from mean levels.

Normal Distribution Curve

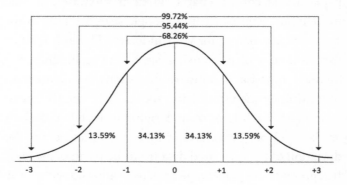

NORMAL DISTRIBUTION CURVE

Six Sigma, (expressed as range between -3 sigma and + 3 sigma in the horizontal axis in diagram above) mainly applicable to larger organisations, was first set up by Motorola in late 1980s along with the help of Dr Juran. Motorola indicated savings of $17 billion over fifteen years due to implementation of Six Sigma across the company. Similar savings were achieved in General Electric and Honeywell and many others. Please refer to any society of quality /or learn Six Sigma to understand more.

What is the Cost of Quality?

Any wastage happening due to lack of quality is the cost of quality, and there are costs in all wastes:

- Loss of product – The cost is calculated as Material plus labour plus Overhead plus margin lost due to rejected product.

- Rework – Costs include labour (hiring QC inspectors to stop the wastage) and material (reordering of material)
- Delays in supply – Loss of credibility in the eyes of the customer leads to lower sales.
- Hiring of extra NVAP to inspect line quality instead of teaching and providing tools to the VAP on line

It is important to recognize that quality means life cycle costs, not just purchase cost. Life cycle cost is the total cost of the labour, material and equipment incurred during the life of the same, which includes purchase cost plus commissioning costs plus cost of maintenance/service during its life plus cost of failure or non-availability of the line due to breakdowns plus spare parts replacement costs. Cheap equipment may have very high lifecycle costs and so will be a totally counter productive investment. By capturing /quantifying the cost of waste in quality you can then undertake root cause analysis and justify changes and investments that address this.

Continuous Improvement

Every organisation will gain tremendously by implementing the philosophy of continuous improvement in their processes. Kaizen, a two-word Japanese phrase meaning *change* ("kai") and meaning *for better* ("zen") was established by Masaaki Imai, who also established Kaizen Institute who indicated that "since introducing this term as a systematic approach for business improvement, companies that implement KAIZEN™ have continually yielded superior results." The principle behind continuous improvements is that every step-in business processes can be improved to achieve better outcomes, lesser costs, and be more effective by following of the principles as laid out by Masaaki Imai. (You can read more about kaizen in the famous book or visit the link https://www.kaizen.com/.)

Developed by Shewhart and promoted heavily by Deming is the Plan-Do-Check-Act technique, a very common method used for continuous learning and improvement leading to effective problem-solving.

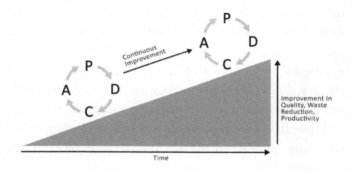

PDCA DIAGRAM. CREDITS-
SHEWHART AND DEMING.

The diagram shows that if you use the PDCA technique to improve your quality, productivity, and costs, with time you will see higher quality, higher productivity and produce lower-cost products or services. Continual application of PDCA at these higher levels will increase all three aspects further and you can keep moving up the incline.

When you promise quality products, you make the promise for all products and services. Your customer expects a certain level of consistency in your products and services. If you like to drink coffee or tea, you always want every cup you buy or make to taste exactly the same. How disappointing it would be if you went to buy coffee at a shop and got coffee that tasted different or was made from a different quality of roasted beans. You would leave the café and go find the place and barista who gives you exactly the coffee taste you like. If they don't change anything, then you will continue buying coffee there forever. It is the same thing with your buyers: they want the same quality every time they buy from you. So not only they are looking at the quality they want, but they are also looking at consistency in the quality. If you start giving them varying quality product, that is, inconsistent product and services, you will lose them very quickly. Consistency of delivered quality says more than only quality products; that is the mainstay of your business with any customer.

For further study please see the book resources list in Further Reading, numbers 5, 15, 16, 17, 18, 19, 20, 21

RULE 26

BECOME GOOD AT SALES AND MARKETING.

*"You can have everything in life you want,
if you will just help enough other people
get what they want." —Zig Ziglar*

Understanding sales and marketing is crucial to your success. It is not a new skill for anyone. Everyone engages in the selling of ideas to get what they want. Throughout your life, from childhood to maturity, you have sold your ideas to all around you—your parents, family, friends, spouse—be it getting your parents to buy you ice-cream, or convincing your spouse to let you buy that car, if you have been successful it is because you applied sales and marketing techniques well.

In a business environment, sales and marketing are critical to the business' survival so it is crucial you excel at it or hire people who do.

What is the difference between sales and marketing?

Sales is defined as the activity of selling of goods and services which result in revenue. It involves the process steps of:

- Lead generation – creating a prospect
- Conversion – the prospect's conversion to a potential customer
- Deal – closing the sale
- Actual Sales transaction – Money is exchanged for product or service
- Continuity of business – repeat sales and development of long-term customers

Marketing is defined as creating interest in the consumers for your products and services. Marketing is a brand promotion exercise which helps grow the sales. Successful marketing campaigns lead to actual revenue and, hence, they are strongly related. Brand promotions and social media are marketing activities that create sales revenue. Marketing today is considered building your brand more than anything else.

There are hundreds of knowledgeable resources available to master sales and marketing techniques. At the end of this chapter, I have indicated some iconic books that you should read to improve your skills and knowledge. Here, however, I want to underline the importance of understanding the concepts of *value proposition* and *job to be done*.

Value Proposition

No business planning is possible without understanding the meaning and purpose of this concept. Value proposition is the reason why customers keep coming back for your products and service. The customers perceive that the particular product or service provides value for the price they pay in meeting the Job To Be Done by the product or service (see also next heading).

Strategyzer has developed a great tool to define the value proposition as overcoming the 'pains' and providing the 'gains' for the customer's Job-to-be-done. Using the Value Proposition Canvas as below helps provide the definite product or service design and can be downloaded at https://www.strategyzer.com/resources/canvas-tools-guides.

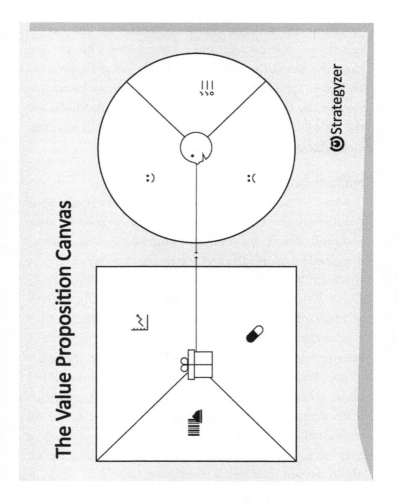

STRATEGYZER'S VALUE PROPOSITION
CANVAS. (Reproduced with permission)

Value Proposition Canvas is a tool for marketing experts, product owners, and value creators. This method from the bestselling innovation book Value Proposition Design is applied in leading organizations and start-ups worldwide. Please click on the link to download and see the video on how to set it up: https://www.strategyzer. com/library/the-value-proposition-canvas

Job To Be Done

Job To Be Done is a concept that will change your product's or service offering's market acceptance, its price and profitability, and your value proposition. The concept, discussed by many sales and marketing experts, was put in this form by Anthony W. Ulwick in his book *Jobs To Be Done: Theory to Practice* and by Prof Clayton Christensen of Harvard in his book The Innovator's Solution. This was recognised "as the first time the product innovation became a science" as put forth by Phillip Kotler, the father of sales and marketing. (For a free download of the JBTD book, please visit https://jobs-to-be-done-book.com/.) In brief, Anthony says all buying decisions are based on emotional, social, and rational bases, in that order. You may be in need of a pen, but you go searching for an expensive pen to ensure it meets your emotional need ("it looks and feels good in my pocket") and social need ("I can impress my friends that I have good and expensive tastes"). You buy a car because you like its looks and colour and feel great driving it, rather than considering the price first. You splurge on things just because you feel happy owning them, not just because they do the job you want them to do. So, if you create an emotional attachment to your product or service, you will be able to create a great market for your product. Toyota sells cars using its "Oh what a feeling" ad and has the highest car market share in the world. You will see a lot of examples that portray the emotional or social attraction rather than rational.

Handling the Competition

Every organisation has to face competition, and you will have to sell your goods and services against them. Competition is a very good thing to happen to you. There is only one way to handle the competition:

HANDLING THE COMPETITION

See the picture above. A person is pointing towards his brain to show that you need to use your brain and intelligence to handle competition. Competition is good for you as it makes you think differently and makes you overcome the low sales and profits problems against the market forces.

Steps to become better than your competitors:

1. Analyse the target market where you want to sell – continually research, research, and research.
2. Conduct benchmarking against the competition on costs and prices. Use Google Analytics to collect data quickly.
3. There are many resources available from the respective industry membership bodies and market research companies like IBIS (www.ibis.com.au), MINTEL (www.mintel.com), and Euromonitor (www.euromonitor.com) etc that provide data to help you.
4. Understand the concepts of Job To Be Done and Value Proposition as explained above.
5. Understand the strategic business planning process for your long-term growth (see Rule 27 and the Business Plan Canvas below).

USE STRATEGIC BUSINESS PLANNING.

No business can grow consistently and profitably without putting together a three- to five-year strategic business plan. Preparing a budget for sales every year is not a strategic business plan. There is far more to growth of a business, and multiplying revenue and profit happens only by planning and deciding what actions are required. Many companies do not involve widely within the organisation and go through the process of preparing a strategic plan with their teams. This rule will help you understand the subject of strategic planning and execution so you can contribute to the success on this to your top management even if you are not getting exposed to the process.

Business Model Canvas

My preferred best method for preparing a strategic business plan starts with using the business model canvas of Strategyzer (https://www.strategyzer.com/). This tool is the most powerful and effective tool I have used to teach and implement business planning. You can download the business canvas at the website https://www.strategyzer.com/canvas/business-model-canvas. There is great video to explain how to use it and develop the canvas, which is shown below:

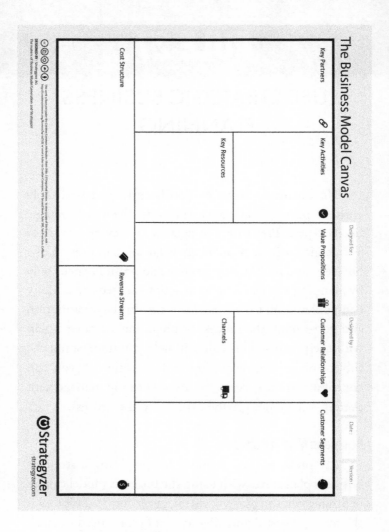

STRATEGYZER'S BUSINESS MODEL
CANVAS. (Reproduced with permission).

Strategic Business Plan (SBP)

The difference between a sales budget and the SBP is in the depth and the details of activities that are involved in achieving the goals that the business has established. The difference is explained in the table below.

Strategic Business Plan vs. Sales Budget

Strategic Business Plan (SBP)	Sales Budget
The SBP is aspirational in nature and reflects what the business wants to achieve in its strategic goals.	The sales budget always looks at sales revenue. It does not reflect completely what organisation wants or needs to achieve to grow.
The SBP is always prepared on a long-term basis, and generally covers the next three to five years, year by year.	The sales budget is mostly planned sales revenue on a short-term basis and generally for the next year.
The SBP drives the growth in revenue, profitability, operational growth, assets acquisition, capital investment, people needed, etc	The sales budget drives only the sales revenue. Other activities to achieve that revenue are not visible to all.
The SBP helps define the activities based on the purpose of the business. Often, it actually helps keep the focus on the purpose.	Purpose of the business is not clear in the sales budget document.
The SBP prioritizes its resources towards increase in return on investment	The Sales Budget guides capital investment decisions but this is not presented as part of the budget document.

The SBP execution is done with all the people working in the organisation. The failure or success of it depends upon company culture.	The sales budget is driven by sales and marketing people who may or may not be involved in other parts of the organisation.

Strategic Business Plan on a page: Below is a great example of preparing SBP for top level in one page to convey it organisation wide.

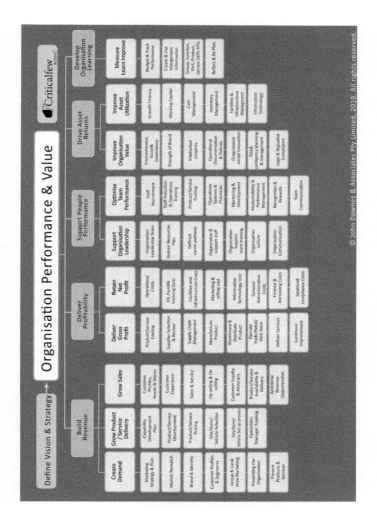

ONE-PAGE STRATEGIC BUSINESS PLAN

Developed by John Downes, the image besides shows a detailed A3 sheet enabling you to build, as he calls it Organisation Performance & Value framework, which is in three layers. At the top is the Vision and Mission level. The second layer shows the strategic goals: Build Revenue, Deliver Profitability, Support People Performance, Drive Assets Returns, and Develop Organisation. The boxes in the layer below are the action triggers under each of the goals to allow you to create action plans. You go through each box and write down your thoughts for the business (or your section) and so create the list covering the next 3-5 years. You can also go to https://www.criticalfewactions.com.au/ to do this online. There may be some costs involved and you will get a report conveying gaps in each of the action plans across the organisation.

Documenting the SBP leads to the next step: Execution. The SBP has no meaning if we cannot execute it. The best resource for understanding this is *Execution: The Discipline of Getting Things Done* by Larry Bossidy and Ram Charan, explained at this link: https://youexec.com/book-summaries/execution-the-discipline-of-getting-things-done. As per the book

"Execution requires a comprehensive understanding of a business, its people, and its environment." The leader must be in charge of getting things done by running the three core processes – picking other leaders, setting the strategic direction, and conducting operations." In other words, you need the strategy, right people and proper operations first to execute any implementation.

RULE 28

MAKE YOUR WORKPLACE OPERATIONS SAFE.

Making your workplace safe is the most critical responsibility for management. We must ensure a safe working environment for workers across all the locations they work in, period. Every person who comes to work must safely return home to their family every time. Anyone injured at work is the responsibility of the company always, and this is bound by law in every country. In some countries, like Australia, management can be jailed for failure to maintain safe environments, procedures, training, equipment, and processes to manage safety. Occupational Health and Safety (OHS) is a very crucial part of management control, performance monitoring, and implementation.

Workplace safety regulations lay out the framework to be followed, which includes:

- records of incidents, including near misses
- injury investigation reports
- provision of adequate safety guards and equipment
- return-to-work programmes for injured employees
- provision of first aid and other equipment on site, like defibrillators and trained first aid officers to cover all shifts and genders.
- safety committee formation and meeting actions

- monthly KPIs for number of injuries, such as extent of seriousness (Lost Time due to Injuries-LTI) and frequency of occurrences, benchmarked against your industry. See Rule 17 for KPIs under safety. Please also see the LTI graph in case study in Rule 11.

Understand Near Misses

A *near miss* is defined as an incident that happens but does not actually cause an injury or property damage. We tend to ignore and overlook such incidents as the dropping of a tool on the floor, the placement of a hazard in the middle of pathway, removal of a guard on a machine, failure to follow the set procedure, or shortcuts that do not cause actual incidents to require investigation.

Heinrich conducted a study way back in 1920s on injury claims and created an eye-opening chart. He found that the there was a pattern to the level of injuries sustained in an organisation as below.

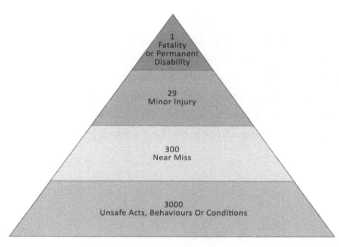

NEAR MISS TRIANGLE OF SAFETY.

Diagram courtesy of https://www.ishn.com/articles/109182-the-safety-triangle-a-useful-yet-complicated-theory.

Explanation: Depending upon the type of industry, for every occurrence of a fatal or serious accident, at least twenty-nine incidents of minor injury or property damage had happened earlier, and before those incidents at least 300 to 600 near misses. In other words, the organisation had the opportunity to look at hundreds of near misses and take action to reduce them before the minor or fatal injury occurred. Called the Safety Triangle Theory, it has guided safe operations strategies for decades.

Controlling near misses, therefore, becomes the most crucial part of safety performance as the numbers convey. It is essential to implement a sustained communication programme to ensure people report near misses; a simple form or QR code requiring minimal details will make it easy to record the incident quickly. Recording the numbers of near misses every month will allow you to keep your incidents below levels where there are more serious injuries and property damage. Businesses I have consulted with have found the QR Code system to be very good, facilitating quick recording and reflection.

CONCLUSION

When I look at the finished book, I feel proud that I have been able to put out what I feel is a handy tool and reference book that you can use to rise out of the middle management role into higher roles and to greater achievements, even into board membership.

The idea for this book came about when I was sitting one day in Melbourne with my great friend and fellow business adviser Bruno Bello, like we have done over the years, discussing the issues faced by our clients. Now, over some time, I had been writing down in my phone a list of issues faced by the company managers and SME owners. I showed it to Bruno. He suggested I write a book on how to help them address those issues in the list. My first list was about fifteen points, which expanded to these 28 rules, and so here you find them in this book.

I decided that the book had to be a handy pocketbook size, the best reference book possible in the world on the various subjects that I knew about and had learnt from. I wanted to include the various comments and sayings that had helped me overcome difficult times, especially share those that helped me escape the rat race faced by managers every day.

I set out the book on the same principles and steps that I have grown with. Everything I say here in this book has been used by me with success. There is nothing written in this book that I have either not used or followed.

I also wanted you, the reader, to answer questions relevant to each rule indicated so that you think about how you can improve your organisation. The questions should invoke actions to resolve the issues raised.

Another suggestion came from another good friend, Gus Cantone (a retired ex CEO), who suggested I make a table of issues that links to the rules for the various solutions to the problems. That table serves as a quick look-up reference to the problems you face. I also read a lot, so I wanted to ensure I provided the list of the reading resources I refer to within the book; they contributed to my knowledge and the authors are masters of their subjects. Many of these authors are world famous and have sold hundreds of thousands of copies so I don't have any hesitancy in sharing these resources. As a leader you need to be a reader; you will not regret forming this habit.

Hopefully, through this book, you have been able to understand and improve yourself, and it has helped you create staff engagement and is guiding you in business management with increasing knowledge. I thank the resources I have mentioned and the persons behind them and am sure you will also gain from these learnings.

DISCLAIMER

The advice and guidance provided in this book, are based on the author's experience and research. While every effort has been made to ensure the accuracy and effectiveness of the information, success in implementing these suggestions cannot be guaranteed. Success will come from your own efforts made after correct understanding of the contents and taking all due care to implement the contents in the correct way after carrying out further research as needed. The author and publisher disclaim any liability for any loss or risk, personal or otherwise, resulting from the use of the information in this book.

FURTHER READING

1) *The Magic of Thinking Big* by David J. Schwartz
2) *Execution: The Discipline of Getting Things Done* by Larry Bossidy and Ram Charan
3) *ChEQmate: Using Corporate Held Emotional Intelligence as a Winning Business Strategy* by Fritz Shoemaker
4) *Principle-Centred Leadership* by Stephen R. Covey
5) *Jugaad Innovation: Think Frugal, Be Flexible, Generate Breakthrough Growth* by Jaideep Prabhu, Navi Radjou, and Dr Simone Ahuja
6) *Personality Plus: How to Understand Others by Understanding Yourself* by Florence Littauer
7) *Start with Why* by Simon Sinek
8) Steve Jobs by Walter Isaacson
9) *Bill Gates: A Biography by* Michael B. Becraft
10) *Jack: Straight from the Gut* by Jack Welch
11) *Statistical method from the viewpoint of quality control* by Walter A. Shewhart and W. Edwards Deming
12) Management statistical books or various websites by CRC Press (https://www.routledge.com/), also known as A Productivity Press, part of Taylor & Francis Group.
13) *Understanding Variation: The Key to Managing Chaos* by Donald J. Wheeler

14) *Memory Jogger: A Pocket Guide of Tools for Continuous Improvement*, edited by Michael Brassard

15) Toyota Production System (TPS), at <u>https://global.toyota/en/company/vision-and-philosophy/production-system/</u>

16) *Toyota Production System: Beyond Large-Scale Production* by Taiichi Ohno

17) *Books* by Eliyahu M. Goldratt*: "Goal" and "Theory of Constraints"*

18) *A Revolution in Manufacturing: The SMED System* by Shigeo Shingo

19) *Zero Quality Control: Source Inspection and the Poka-Yoke System* by Shigeo Shingo

20) *Kaizen and The Art of Creative Thinking: The Scientific Thinking Mechanism* by Shigeo Shingo

21) *Fundamental Principles of Lean Manufacturing* by Shigeo Shingo

22) *Scaling Up: How to Build a Meaningful Business and Enjoy the Ride* by Verne Harnish

23) *APICS Operations Management Body of Knowledge Framework*, at <u>http://www.apics.org/docs/default-source/industry-content/apics-ombok-framework.pdf</u>

24) Various books marketing and sales by Phillip Kotler, also considered as father of modern marketing, an American marketing author, consultant, and professor emeritus; the S. C. Johnson & Son Distinguished Professor of International Marketing at the Kellogg School

of Management at Northwestern University (1962–2018).

25) Books by Brian Tracy, Chairman & CEO of Brian Tracy International and author of fifty-five books translated into forty-two languages. Please see https://www.briantracy.com/.

26) Books by Zig Ziglar, author of over thirty books including *See You at the Top,* still in print. See https://www.ziglar.com/.

27) Nakajima, Seiichi (1988). Introduction to TPM: Total Productive Maintenance.

28) Hansen, Robert C (2005). Overall Equipment Effectiveness (OEE).

29) Koch, Arno (2007). OEE for the Production Team.

30) Say Yes to your Potential – Skip Ross Magic Formula for Dynamic Living by Skip Ross and Carole Carlson

31) *Jobs To Be Done: Theory to Practice* (published 2016) *by Anthony W. Ulwick:*

32) Rich Dad Poor Dad by Robert Kiyosaki

33) Maverick by Ricardo Semmler

34) Seven Habits of Highly Effective People by Steven Covey

35) Grow your factory, grow your profits by Tim Mclean

36) Working with Emotional Intelligence by Daniel Goleman

This list is by no means complete and there are so many other sources also available. I like further readings from

Harvard Business Review, professional bodies like Australian Institute of Directors (AICD), professional membership associations, research institutes like CSIRO, academic papers from other universities etc. Due diligence and research should always be done to increase the subject knowledge.

Vineet has a passion for manufacturing and operations improvement, helping businesses to achieve their aspirations along with personal growth in leadership and governance for the business owners and their senior management. He has working experience from operational floor level to advisory boards, covering 47 years of management in implementing excellence in oil, plastics, chemicals, food, pet food, confectionary, health foods, medical devices, healthcare products, and working in global icons companies to small company in partnership. With direct experience of advisory, production, procurement, planning, logistics, quality, business development, technical sales & services, engineering, consulting and project management, Vineet is a "thinker-doer mentor" with high people skills and strong customer service orientation.

Vineet has technical and leadership skills with achievements in organizational transformations of loss-making businesses of global icons, improving business growth, increasing profits, reducing costs and waste, developing people to achieve "HIGHER," turning around morale and businesses, improving safety, influencing cultural change for continuous improvement and setting up self-managed teams, teaching and mentoring senior managers to set and execute strategies across the organizations. His achievements are also spread across implementing best practices in manufacturing, business development, consulting to Australian & global companies, representing USA technology companies in Australia and technology transfer projects in Malaysia, India and Mexico.

As an adviser, Vineet helps businesses to expand markets, take advantage of government incentives, grants and assistance, running networking groups for alliance and collaboration across the SMEs.

Vineet is a qualified Mechanical Engineer, holds an MBA, a PG Dip in Quality Management, as well as being a TAE40110 qualified trainer and a mentor.

Specialties:
Advising start-ups to large SMEs
Strategic business plans and execution

Value Proposition

Developer of RAAT tool (Responsibility, Accountability, Authority, Trust)

Continuous Improvement Projects and LEAN

Changing culture

Business turnarounds

Business financial analysis and foundations for profitability, costings, cashflow

Project management, plant layouts, process optimization

Conversion to running by self-directed/self-managed TEAMs.

Mentoring all levels, shop floor to senior managers,

Coaching & training on operational excellence & certificates I to IV

Restructuring into flatter organizations.

Manufacturing management: procurement, inventory, planning, engineering, quality, warehouse

LinkedIn Profile: https://www.linkedin.com/in/vineet-ahuja-9720403/

9 780228 895039